Public Planning

PUBLIC PLANNING:
Failure
and Redirection

ROBERT A. LEVINE

Basic Books, Inc., Publishers

NEW YORK / LONDON

© 1972 by Basic Books, Inc.
Library of Congress Catalog Card Number 72–76913
SBN 465–06777–8
Manufactured in the United States of America

Preface

The thesis of this book is that public programs in the United States have not worked well in the past, nor do they in the present. The major reason suggested for this outcome is that programs designed to fulfill policy objectives are laid out by planners for operation by administrators, with the administrators fulfilling the plan by following a hierarchy of rules. The planners and administrators at the top lay out the basic rules as general guidelines; the middle-level administrators make them into detailed rules of procedure; the operators at the bottom must apply them by interpretations based on administrative discretion. In this process of interpretation the original policy objectives more often than not get lost or even reversed. Ordinarily they are changed around not by malfeasance but by honest attempts at interpretation, with each attempt a little bit off and the cumulated result far from the intended objective of the public program.

My contention, then, is that in order to advance policy objectives through public programs effectively, the attempt should be made to use individual and organizational incentives to interpret policies down to operating levels, using rules much less than is done now. The market system is one example of the use of incentives instead of rules in order to move in a socially desirable direction—the profit incentive to move toward greater production in the case of the private market. It is suggested here that market techniques might be used to reach a range of public objectives as well as private production; government action can provide a profitable market to bring private resources into education or manpower training, for example. But market techniques are not the only ones; the objectives designated by public policy may be furthered by changing the structure of bargaining or political power, as happened when the New Deal legitimized collective bargaining. Within public bureaucracies, bureaucratic incentives might be used, although less is known about bureaucratic motivations than either market or political incentives.

This stress on incentives is related to but differs from some of the current emphasis on decentralization. Decentralization of the administration of public policies is likely to work very poorly indeed if the decentralization is not coupled with incentives to induce the decentralized parts to work toward common objectives. If anything, decentralization under rules is likely to work less well than centralization under rules, because the rules for decentralized operations are necessarily looser and more liable to unintended reversal by discretion.

The above is a very rough summary of some of the major points made in this book. These ideas can be applied to a number of current proposals for reorganization of the administration of public programs—proposals that, although they are current, are likely to be under discussion for quite a while. Chief among these are the Nixon administration's proposals for revenue-sharing—the provision of funds gathered in by federal taxation for expenditure at the discretion of states and localities. Revenue-sharing proposals are of two types—general revenue-sharing, which would provide federal funds with no guidelines as to what they should be spent for, and special revenue-sharing, under which broad areas for expenditure, like education or health, are specified. Although there are important distinctions between these two concepts, my overall comments here apply to both.

Revenue-sharing proposals are designed to reach two objectives, one short-run, the other long. The short-run aim, to meliorate the fiscal crisis that has hit some states and many local jurisdictions, is not the subject here. The other idea behind revenue sharing, however, is more relevant to the material in this study. It is that local officials have knowledge of local problems that enables them to be more effective in carrying out functions that had previously been carried out either by the federal government or by local government under relatively stringent federal guidelines. That locals know their own problems better than the feds is perhaps true, but the importance of this truth depends on its interpretation. Does it mean that there should be no (or many fewer) national policies and that local officials should choose both the directions and emphases in policy areas that until now have been thought to be in the national sphere? Maybe so, but if this is the interpretation, it leaves me with a number of doubts. One obvious national policy many people hope will not be abdicated is the drive toward desegregation. They (and I) doubt that the question of whether to desegregate should be returned to the states. Parallel to this and perhaps slightly less obvious is the problem of poverty. Some years ago, a national decision was made to adopt as a national goal the reduction of and perhaps the end to poverty in the United States. Should the question of whether this is a valid objective be left to states and localities? My own background in the poverty program leads me to oppose this; too many states and localities have ignored the problems of poverty for too long.

This leads to the other possible interpretation of the fundamental objective of revenue-sharing—revenue-sharing not as a way of letting states and localities choose broad policy objectives, but of executing more effectively policies still determined nationally. Here, too, I have severe doubts. For if national policies are to be executed by state and local governments, lower jurisdictions must somehow be impelled to work in the nationally desired direction. As suggested above, rules are not likely to be very effective in moving their interpreters in the desired directions. (Title I of the education act, for example, which can be considered an existing example of special revenue-sharing, has been quite ineffective in improving the education of the underprivileged children it was supposed to help.) Manipulation of incentives might move operations in the directions desired by policy, but here we come up against the hard barrier of our lack of knowledge about what incentives work for officials of local government, whether politicians or bureaucrats. Some simple ideas do not really seem to be applicable. Local officials are not out to maximize the inflow of federal funds nor even to minimize local taxes. Their objectives have much more to do with aiding or reducing burdens upon particular constituencies in patterns we simply know very little about. Looking at the current local administration of Public Assistance, for example, minimization of local tax burdens is surely important, but it is hardly all. Also entering the complex are mixed feelings of charity and puritan justice that lead local governments to do some very unexpected things with welfare. In this area, as in others, there is very little reason to believe that national policy has been or can be effectively administered by local authority.

Indeed, in the welfare area, the Nixon administration has, through its Family Assistance proposals, tried to move in the direction of more centralized national administration, a direction different from that of its revenue-sharing proposals. My own feeling is that while centralization is not the answer for everything, decentralization without an understanding of the incentives of those to whose control a program is to be decentralized is likely to help little. Indeed, one wonders why the administration, instead of turning to the decentralized federalism of revenue-sharing, did not turn instead to the incentive-guided decentralization and competition of the market system as a device for implementing public policy. (We *do* know a lot about the workings of the profit incentive.) Turning to the market ought to be at least as natural for a Republican administration as turning to the states, yet little has been done in that direction. There have been a few experimental attempts to use market devices and some emphasis on using business "know-how" for public ends. Yet the most attractive thing about utilizing the private economy for public ends is not business know-how, which can foul things up quite as badly as public know-how, but the market itself, which tends to select out those businesses that do, in fact, know how better than do their competitors. The private market, unlike most public systems, achieves its objectives through the profit-induced competition of multiple producers.

It seems likely that such turning to market and similar devices might be a strong political possibility for the future, for either a Republican or Democratic administration. What is suggested here should be relatively neutral in terms of party ideology.

Indeed, the other criticism of a current administrative proposal made here is quite explicitly neutral, politically—it concerns a proposal made in different forms by both the Johnson and Nixon administrations. This is the idea of reducing the number of cabinet departments down to a few "super departments" ranging over broad substantive areas. President Johnson suggested consolidation of the Departments of Commerce and Labor; President Nixon has recommended other consolidations. Yet here is a case where the same ideas which lead to doubts about decentralization to states and localities lead to other doubts about greater centralization within the federal government. The connecting thread is not centralization or decentralization; it is competition and incentives. Decentralization to states and localities induces no competition; the State of California is a public monopoly, having a different geographical jurisdiction from Nevada, a different juridical jurisdiction from Los Angeles County.

Within a single jurisdiction, however, bureaucratic competition is more likely to engender effective implementation of public policy than is the consolidation recommended by Messrs. Johnson and Nixon. The administrations proposing such consolidation have done so in the name of omitting overlap and duplication—a fine old-fashioned bureaucratic principle. Yet it is a principle that has never really worked to make policy effective; the opposite concept, that of competition, has worked very well to make the private economy productive. The question to be asked, then, is Why not encourage overlapping and duplication and try to get public bureaucracies operating more effectively by the incentives induced by such competition? Again, my background in the poverty program—the OEO experiment of the Johnson administration—pushes my views in this direction. OEO achieved a number of things by competing with "old line" government agencies in fields they thought they had monopolized. As in the private market, the fresh air of competition frequently worked very effectively.

In any case, that is what this study is about—how to make public policy effective by use of decentralization guided by incentives, by centralization where called for, by competition, where possible. The study has benefited greatly by extensive comments from a number of people: Kathleen Archibald, Harvey Averch, William Capron, Yehezkel Dror, Morton Halperin, Bertrand Harding, William Jones, Joseph Kershaw, Anthony Pascal, Richard Rainey, Henry Rowen, Albert Williams and Walter Williams. Most of the work was funded by a grant from the Ford Foundation. Thanks for all this assistance is gratefully extended; responsibility for views and interpretations remains with the author.

1972   R.A.L.

Contents

Public Planning

1   Introduction

THE VIEWPOINT of this book is that most public programs in the United States have not worked well; some have not worked at all. Whether one defines "not working well" as failure to solve the problems for which public action is appropriate, failure to substantially improve the situation beyond what it would have been without the programs, or (a criterion that in a sense summarizes the others) failure of programs to live up to the reasonable expectations of their designers, most public programs have not worked well.

To explain this failure, one could blame the public planning process for not coming to grips with the realities of politics and bureaucracies in laying out programs, or one could blame the operation of the programs for failure to follow plans. In any case, a major gap between needs and expectations on the one side and program achievement on the other side exists.

The effort here, then, is to examine empirically this gap between expectations and achievements, to analyze its causes, and to suggest ways of narrowing it by improving achievements. The result, however, is not a general theory of public planning. For one thing, the evidence used is for planning and policy-making in the United States alone, and the generalizations are thus applicable only to the United States. It is frequently contended that planning has succeeded in smaller nations (Israel, the Netherlands, Scandinavia); to the extent that the contention can be borne out, it seems likely that success is due in large measure to smallness. At any rate, the United States, with its still-heterogeneous society and economy and its federal form of government, seems different enough to start within these national confines.

This leads to the second limit on generalization. The emphasis here is on national policy (including national policy for locally determined programs), and the viewpoint is that of high-level national policy-makers and planners. This does not mean the problems of the Presidency, which are unique, but the policy problems of those in Washington and elsewhere whose job it is to carry out the programs necessarily laid out only in broad outline by the chief executive, and who may advise him on these programs. It is important to point this out at the outset because, just as solutions applicable to the Netherlands may not be applicable to the United States, solutions that work for a corporation or for a unit of a public bureaucracy are not necessarily applicable to the making of policy for the United States. Indeed, this will be one of the major sources of difficulty discussed in this study, that even though substantial increases in efficiency may be available to small units, the high-level policy-maker looking down at myriads of small units cannot readily get them to adopt these efficient modes of action. Planning at these high levels is thus quite different and more difficult; yet its success is necessary to the successful carrying out of public programs from bottom to top. That is the problem.

The word "planning" has been assigned many definitions. The one used here is among the broadest: "Planning" is the advance laying out of a program of actions. "Implementation" can then be defined as the carrying out of a program of actions.

Planning and implementation, however, though definitionally separable, are closely intertwined. Planning must concern itself with implementation; one major difficulty with public planning to date is that it has demanded implementation of a sort that could not be delivered. And both planning and implementation have demanded of political decision-makers what they would not deliver. These failures of planners and implementers to understand one another's motivations and limitations, and the failure of both to understand the political context in which they operate, are at the root of the overall problem. Thus, though this is a book about planning, the heart of the discussion centers on examples of different modes of implementing public policy. If policy can be implemented effectively, it can be planned; and though the converse of this statement is true by definition (if policy can be planned effectively it can be implemented) the latter statement is trivial, because policy cannot be planned effectively without knowing how to implement it.

Planning has only recently come into a major role in U.S. government operations. Of course, in the sense of the above definition—laying out some course to be followed—public planning has always been done; even the most existential of public policy-makers has to think at least a little bit in advance of what happens next. But formal, self-conscious, and comprehensive planning in government, concerning actions and objectives in a number of functional fields, is more recent. It seems accurate to say that though such comprehensive self-conscious public planning was attempted in some states (for example, Wisconsin) during the early twentieth century and was widely discussed at the federal level during the 1930s, it became really pervasive at the federal level and below only during the 1960s.

At the federal level, the manifest of the triumph of the planning ethos was the institution in 1965 of the Planning, Programming, and Budgeting (PPB) system throughout the federal government by directive of President Johnson implemented by the Bureau of the Budget. The system, which had been introduced to the federal government in 1961 in the Department of Defense by Secretary Robert McNamara and Assistant Secretary Charles Hitch, was deemed so successful that it was to be instituted government-wide.

The planning ethos spread not only through the federal government, but by federal action, to local instrumentalities funded partly or in full by the federal government. The requirement for local antipoverty plans under the Community Action Program of the War on Poverty was perhaps the first widely known example of such a federal requirement for comprehensive local planning. But the requirements for a "workable program" under public housing and urban renewal legislation [1] and the availability of federal grants both for urban and rural planning under urban planning legislation antedated Community Action, and somewhat narrower planning in such fields as highway construction and water resource projects is an older requirement. The lack of comprehensiveness in highway planning, its concentration on efficient transportation at the cost of community and environmental factors, has been the basis of one of the major criticisms of this planning. In any case, once Community Action began the process of federal encouragement of more comprehensive local planning on a large scale (and failed to produce meaningful plans at the local level), it was followed by bigger and better or at least different planning requirements under Model Cities legislation.

That the hopes for planning were high indeed is shown by the language with which President Johnson announced the original PPB system in August 1965:

This morning I have just concluded a breakfast meeting with the Cabinet and with the heads of Federal agencies and I am asking each of them to immediately begin to introduce a very new and a very revolutionary system of planning and programming and budgeting throughout the vast Federal Government, so that through the tools of modern management the full promise of a finer life can be brought to every American at the lowest possible cost.

Under this new system each Cabinet and agency head will set up a very special staff of experts who, using the most modern methods of program analysis, will define the goals of their department for the coming year. And once these goals are established this system will permit us to find the most effective and the least costly alternative for achieving American goals.

This program is designed to achieve three major objectives: it will help us find new ways to do jobs faster, to do jobs better and to do jobs less expensively. It will insure a much sounder judgment through more accurate information, pinpointing those things that we ought to do more, spotlighting those things that we ought to do less. It will make our decision-making process as up-to-date, I think, as our space-exploring programs.

Everything that I have done in both legislation and the construction of a budget has always been guided by my own very deep concern for the American people, consistent with wise management, of course, of the taxpayer's dollar. So this new system will identify our national goals with precision and will do it on a continuing basis. It will enable us to fulfill the needs of all the American people with a minimum amount of waste.

And because we will be able to make sounder decisions than ever before, I think the people of this nation will receive greater benefits from every tax dollar that is spent in their behalf.[2]

And even after four years of very mixed experience with the PPB system, the strength of the planning ethos was such that the hopes remained high. In May 1969, Senator William Proxmire, chairman of the Subcommittee on Economy in Government of the Congressional Joint Economic Committee, wrote that:

> The absence of partisan dispute over the use of PPB points to the recognition by responsible Government officials that we must be rational in our approach to public policy decisions. For, to use PPB to obtain information about the gains and losses to be anticipated from a decision is to demand no more than that the decision be rational. Properly defined, PPB is the most basic and logical planning tool which exists: it provides for the quantitative evaluation of the economic benefits and the economic costs of program alternatives, both now and in the future, in relation to analyses of similar programs.[3]

Yet this was in spite of the fact that Robert Haveman, the director of Senator Proxmire's study on "The Analysis and Evaluation of Public Expenditures," wrote that:

> From the outset, the PPB System has encountered serious obstacles which impeded improvements in the public decision process. Among the primary impediments which have been cited by observers of the system are the following:
>
> The failure of many agency heads to demand program analysis or to use it in decision-making when it was available;
>
> The lack of interest in (and sometimes opposition to) the system by important congressional committees and congressmen;
>
> The failure of much legislation to clearly stipulate program goals and objectives and to provide funds for the collection of followup data and other program appraisal information;
>
> The existence of private interest groups which anticipate that hard and quantitative program evaluation will endanger the size or existence of expenditures which benefit them;
>
> The constraints on substantive and time-consuming policy analysis imposed by the annual budget cycle and process to which the PPB System is tied;

A serious scarcity of analytical personnel in the PPB offices of civilian agencies;

A basic resistance by many Federal employees to economic analysis and the difficult job of program evaluation;

The lack of professional agreement on certain basic analytical issues, such as the appropriate public interest rate for discounting long-lived public investments, the development of shadow prices when outputs are not marketed, the evaluation of expenditures with multiple objectives, and the evaluation of public expenditures in regions or periods of less than full employment;

The lack of adequate data from which to develop measures of the social benefits of outputs and social costs of inputs.[4]

The point is that though planning such as that represented by the PPB system is generally conceded not to have worked well, to have worked less than well specifically in terms of failure to fill the reasonable expectations of the plan designers, the general thrust continues to be toward trying more and better planning rather than stepping back and questioning the whole process.

In fact, I would join in this general thrust. As badly as formal, comprehensive, detailed, and self-conscious planning has failed planners' expectations, it would certainly seem preferable to the only alternative—no planning. But this sort of statement is trivial; the meaningful question is What sort of planning should be done? And my contention is that the concept of how to plan is in serious need of re-examination, a re-examination that in fact has been begun by the Proxmire study and the several dozens of substudies it contains. The problem is that in great measure to date, the formal public planning process has taken on a more restrictive definition than the one used above: "advance laying out of a program of actions." It has taken on the meaning of detailed specification of the objectives of public programs and the steps to be taken to get there. For federal programs, this has meant not merely laying out in advance, but a system by which a master plan (frequently taking little account of the political environment of operations) has set forth the structure and levels of programs; this is supplemented by subordinate plans, and these in turn are supplemented by plans at the operating level—in industries, plants, states, cities, school districts, local communities, neighborhoods, and so on. All these plans have had to be coordinated with one another to ensure consistency. And all have had to be implemented by program operators who may or may not have been in sympathy with the plans, may or may not have even understood them, but in any case will certainly be governed by their own motives and imperatives, both personal and programmatic. This entire system has been connected up in series so that a partial failure of one link—planning or implementation—has meant a partial failure of the whole, and the whole has been governed by the cumulation of such partial failures. It is a wonder that anyone ever thought it might work.

And local planning, though perhaps having fewer levels of organization, has been of the same type and has failed for the same reasons. Plans have been unrealistic politically (for example, land use plans that ignore inevitable strong pressures to change zoning), and have depended on program operators to follow out the intentions of the planners. This may be a shorter chain than the one starting in Washington, but it is no less vulnerable to weak links. And the prestige and pay of federal planners and managers being higher than those for locals, local planning may compensate for having fewer links in the chain by having a larger proportion of weak links.

Furthermore, since public planning has obviously not worked well, the effort has been made to improve it, but to improve it by doing more of the same—by replanning and recapitulating, by proliferating plans of the same sort. For example, the failure of planning in Community Action has not led to a re-examination of the concept of this kind of planning but to the attempt to do the same kind of planning better under Model Cities; the failure of centralized planning has led to decentralized planning with central review, thus preserving the worst features of both systems. We seem to be planning ourselves into a bog of quicksand where each struggle to get out sinks us more deeply.

One solution to all this is to say that since we cannot plan our way to the goals of the new social programs or to the goals

of a foreign policy which is similarly bogged down in unfulfill-
able planning, we ought to abandon these goals or severely
modify them. This, I think, is premature, at least for domestic
policy. Planning toward these goals and even achieving them is
possible, but to accomplish this a new kind of planning is
needed: planning that takes account of the increasingly sophisticated knowledge of how organizations and systems of organizations work. Some of the relevant knowledge has been with us in
one form or another for a long time; the workings of the private market system may be quite relevant for the planning of
public programs. Other kinds of knowledge—studies of ways
political and bureaucratic systems really work, for example—
are much newer and still at the beginning of their development.
Both the older economic analysis of the market systems and the
newer political analysis of politics and bureaucracies are descriptions of the real world; the current failure of public planning lies largely in the fact that it exists in its own world, which
is too far distant from the way things work today.

Planning is in its essence a normative activity; to plan is to
advocate. It is to advocate a particular course of action, to say
that one course is better than an alternative by some standard.
And typically, the norms of current public planning in the
United States, the standards on the basis of which a course is
advocated, are nonconservative. This is not a logical necessity,
but those who have been attracted to planning have in large
measure arrived there because of their desire to institute social
or other public change, and the desire to institute change is not
a conservative one. Planning of public programs is normative
and nonconservative; so is planning of public planning. Such
systems as PPB have been set up to improve public planning
and through such improvement to advance social programming.

In contrast to the normative nature of planning and the nonconservative nature of most recent planning, the best recent
work analyzing the intricacies of public and private organizations as they really exist is more descriptive than normative;
where norms are used, they are conservative ones: "This complex system depicted is a pretty good one, let's not tinker too
much."

The oldest of these analyses of the organizational world is the classical public administration model. This is the structural analysis of an organization characterized by a pyramidical organizational chart in which information flows upward and authority flows downward. Lines across the chart are avoided as much as possible. This classical kind of public administration produces such concepts as the differentiation between line and staff, the necessary connection of authority and responsibility, the span of control in which the box on a higher line does not supervise too many boxes on a lower line. It is operated by a set of rules and precepts, and these rules and precepts are the norms to which it adheres. Behind these norms is the desire to avoid overlap, duplication, and confusion. If overlap, duplication, and confusion exist, the system is changed by shifting the boxes and rules.

Whether classical public administration was ever thought to describe reality, it is clear from recent organizational analyses that it does not do so in any real sense. That is, decisions are made as much along informal lines connecting parallel boxes as they are along the formal pyramidical lines, line and staff become much confused, authority depends on a set of motivations and incentives not described by an organizational chart, and so forth. Yet the classical model is important as a description because it is still widely used as a norm. It is the bureaucratic system we learned about in public administration courses in college; it is the military system we learned about at boot camp and OCS. The norms of the classical system—the lack of duplication, overlap, and confusion—are important to planning not because they can be approached but because the belief on the part of many bureaucrats that they are approachable is in itself a real world factor to be considered by planners.

Public administration theory has now moved far beyond this classical model in sophistication. One recent book in the field is Anthony Downs's *Inside Bureaucracy*. Downs defines a bureaucratic organization primarily by four characteristics: (1) large size; (2) dependence on the organization by most members for most of their income; (3) performance evaluation of members of the organization by their superiors (and equals) on the basis of performance in their jobs, rather than evaluation either by such ascribed characteristics as religion and social class or by election; (4) the absence of a market test by which the organization and its members stand or fall on the basis of an objective criterion (profits) externally controlled in large measure.[5] This definition is used throughout this book, except that "bureaucracy" here means public bureaucracy only, except when otherwise indicated. Downs characterizes his concept of bureaucracy as resting on three central hypotheses:

1. Bureaucratic officials (and all other social agents) seek to attain their goals rationally. In other words, they act in the most efficient manner possible given their limited capabilities and the cost of information. Hence all the agents in our theory are utility maximizers. In practical terms, this implies that whenever the cost of attaining any given goal rises in terms of time, effort, or money, they seek to attain less of that goal, other things being equal. Conversely, whenever the cost of attaining a goal falls, they seek to attain more of it.

2. Bureaucratic officials in general have a complex set of goals including power, income, prestige, security, convenience, loyalty (to an idea, an institution, or the nation), pride in excellent work, and desire to serve the public interest. This book postulates five different types of officials, each of which pursues a different subset of the above goals. But regardless of the particular goals involved, every official is significantly motivated by his own self-interest even when acting in a purely official capacity.

3. Every organization's social functions strongly influence its internal structure and behavior, and vice versa. This premise may seem rather obvious, but some organization theorists have in effect contradicted it by focusing their analyses almost exclusively on what happens within an organization.[6]

This description of the bureaucratic world is far closer to reality than either the implicit model used by formal public planners or the classical public administration model. But Downs's objective is not a normative one; it is descriptive and theoretical:

This book will attempt to develop a useful theory of bureaucratic decisionmaking. The theory should enable analysts to predict at least some aspects of bureau behavior accurately, and to incorporate bureaus into a more generalized theory of social decision-making—particularly one relevant to democracies. It would be impossible to solve all the problems involved in this immense and complex field. However, we hope we will solve many, and create a framework upon which solutions to still more may be built by other theorists.[7]

Similar to Downs's but stressing more the processes by which political and bureaucratic decisions are made is the work of Charles E. Lindblom. Like Downs's, Lindblom's work is primarily descriptive, but unlike Downs, it is quite clear that Lindblom likes what he describes. Insofar as the work is normative, the norm is that we have a pretty good system which, if it can be changed at all, should not be changed much. Lindblom's statement of his system and objectives can be taken from the first few pages of *The Intelligence of Democracy:*

A simple idea is elaborated in this book: that people can coordinate with each other without anyone's coordinating them, without a dominant common purpose, and without rules that fully prescribe their relations to each other. . . .

The first striking fact about this simple idea is that although significant examples of coordination through mutual adjustment is the subject of a body of theory in economics, many informed persons either in effect deny that it is possible or treat it as of little consequence. Although no one who once reflects on it will explicitly deny the possibility, habits of thought inhibit the reflection. Gulick has, for example, found only two primary means of coordination in public administration: central direction and common purpose.[8]

And there can be no doubt from reading Lindblom's work that he not only delights in the modeling of a far more sophisticated and realistic system than the central direction he criticizes but feels that his system of mutual adjustment has worked very well indeed.

Thus, neither Downs nor Lindblom is a planner in the works cited here.[9] Neither uses his system to reach the new objectives that typify the goals of social planners, nor do James G. March and Herbert A. Simon, whose work on *Organizations* is seminal in this field.[10] And, conversely, social planners have not used the sophistication of Downs, Lindblom, and March and Simon to relate their plans to reality.

Suppose, then, that we attempt to build normative prescriptions for better planning on the new but rich body of descriptive theory, but do so without accepting the implicit conservatism of Lindblom. Suppose that we feel that the goals of the social planners of the last five to ten years are important, such goals as social justice in the United States and peaceful progress internationally. Or suppose, even more dramatically, that we feel these goals are necessary to preserve certain basic widely shared values. Suppose we feel that domestic and international tranquility are ebbing fast, that the United States is moving toward an irretrievable social polarization, and the world at best toward a dangerously unstable equilibrium. Given these beliefs and fears, successful planning for policies to counteract these trends is a necessity. *And the contention of this book is that to be successful, planning has to change its current simple-minded premise of a world in which planners lay out optimal courses to selected goals, bureaucracies translate these courses into action, and implementation follows as neatly as building construction follows a blueprint. It will have to move toward the sophistication of recent descriptive analyses.*

The need for change in the planning and implementation of public programs is accentuated by a phenomenon outside the scope of bureaucratic analysis, the increasing feeling on the part of people of all sorts that they are helpless against the inexorable movements of immense and faceless public and private machinery. This feeling has been articulated most clearly by the advocates of participatory democracy, harking back to the New England town meeting, but it affects almost every segment of society (with the exception of those few that have power, know it, and are satisfied with it). In large measure it is behind campus revolt, as students opposing current wars feel themselves impotent to change military and foreign policy or even to avoid the conscription that makes them instruments of that policy. The feeling of helplessness applies to Negroes who find it impossible to gain equality; it applies equally to those whites who feel—frequently with some justice—that the faceless machine is using their rights and jobs to compensate blacks.

This is a book about public planning and implementation, not about participatory democracy. Yet the two themes are allied. The kind of planning that has initially failed is the kind that depends on a central authority to implement the plans, with orders being passed down and faithfully executed on down the line. Realizing this failure, recent attempts have been made to decentralize planning; these too have failed. Yet, some variety of decentralization seems a necessary condition for success; central planning is inherently ponderous. And, as it turns out in this study (though, because the study is primarily of something else, the conclusion is not stressed), the most hopeful kinds of decentralized planning are entirely compatible with wide participation. Indeed, they depend on it.

In any case, the question asked is whether we can find new forms of planning that can get us from here to there without the commands of a central authority. Can such systems as those analyzed descriptively in recent works be used normatively to achieve goals that do not automatically stem from the workings of bureaucracies or mutual adjustment?

Planners have delineated noble and necessary goals, and organizational analysts have provided sophisticated descriptions of the world in which we must reach these goals but have tended to ingore the goals. What is missing is the modern Machiavelli who will not only describe to his prince the way the world looks but will address analysis specifically to the question of how the prince can get from where he is to where he wants to go:

> May I trust, therefore, that Your Highness will accept this little gift in the spirit in which it is offered; and if Your Highness will deign to peruse it, you will recognise in it my ardent desire that you may attain to that grandeur which fortune and your own merits presage for you.[11]

And indeed, Machiavelli's objective was to enable the prince to gain for his people social objectives which though different from today's, were true social objectives rather than the single-minded quest for personal power that is sometimes incorrectly ascribed to the first modern student of bureaucracy.

This opportunity must not, therefore, be allowed to pass, so that Italy may at length find her liberator. I cannot express the love with which he would be received in all those provinces which have suffered under these foreign invasions, with what thirst for vengeance, with what steadfast faith, with what love, with what grateful tears. What doors would be closed against him? What people would refuse him obedience? What envy could oppose him? What Italian would withhold allegiance? This barbarous domination stinks in the nostrils of everyone. May your illustrious house therefore assume this task with that courage and those hopes which are inspired by a just cause, so that under its banner our fatherland may be raised up, and under its auspices be verified that saying of Petrarch:

> Valour against fell wrath
> Will take up arms; and be the combat quickly sped!
> For, sure, the ancient worth,
> That in Italians stirs the heart, is not yet dead.[12]

Notes

1. Section 701 of the Housing Act of 1954, as amended.
2. *The New York Times,* August 26, 1965.
3. "The Analysis and Evaluation of Public Expenditures: The PPB System," in a compendium of papers submitted to the Subcommittee on Economy in Government of the Joint Economic Committee, Congress of the United States (Washington, D.C.: Government Printing Office, 1969), vol. 1, p. vi.
4. *Ibid.,* pp. 6–7.
5. Anthony Downs, *Inside Bureaucracy,* A Rand Corporation Research Study (Boston: Little, Brown, 1967), pp. 24–25.
6. *Ibid.,* p. 2.
7. *Ibid.,* p. 1.
8. Charles E. Lindblom, *The Intelligence of Democracy* (New York: The Free Press, 1965), pp. 3–4.
9. Actually Downs is a very powerful planner, but *Inside Bureaucracy* is a purely descriptive and theoretical book.
10. James G. March and Herbert A. Simon, *Organizations* (New York: Wiley, 1958).
11. Niccólo Machiavelli, *The Prince and the Discourses* (New York: Random House, Modern Library, 1940), p. 4.
12. *Ibid.,* p. 98.

2

What Works
and What Doesn't

THE UNITED STATES might be considered a system of relationships made up of subsystems, some public, some private, some mixed. The purpose of this chapter and the following two is to investigate a number of these subsystems to see what can be learned about planning and implementation. What is attempted is to build theory inductively from empirical evidence. The evidence used here is selective, that is, I have selected a few of the almost infinity of public and private subsystems that make up our society. Nonetheless, the evidence is not distorted; it is very difficult to find cases on which to build an opposing theory.

The evidence has two parts: One concerns what does not work in the planning and implementation of such subsystems; the other, what does work, and for what. My contention is that what might be termed a highly administered system—that is, one that attempts to operate through detailed applications of policy on a case by case basis, these applications being levied on one set of people called a clientele by another set of people called officials—will generally fail. Most such systems have failed in the past to fulfill the reasonable expectations of their designers; there is no evidence that they will succeed in the future.

Administered systems need not utilize detailed planning in the sense of laying out future courses of action; many such systems are routine ones in which the future may be considered a linear extension of the present and thus little future-oriented planning is needed. But for those administered systems aimed at reaching a future state different from the present one, planning in the detailed sense is done. And it too generally fails.

The evidence for the failure of highly administered systems also comes in two parts. One, discussed in Chapter 3, stems from the analysis of systems operating within the United States, those relating to domestic policy. If such systems are highly administered, they always seem to fail, and by this token so does the planning for those systems that are planned into the future.

The other part of the evidence on the failure of administration is from those systems relating to military policies or to technological policies operating in a fashion similar to the military ones. It is sometimes argued that such systems—the NASA attempt to put a man on the moon, for example—do work far better than those in the domestic social policy fields and that all we have to do is to apply the planning and management techniques of the military and space programs to domestic policy. Chapter 4 suggests, however, that to the extent that the military-NASA systems do seem to work better, this is due largely to their being measured by criteria not politically applicable to planning and management of social systems. Deterrence, for example, has "worked" because something has *not* happened; domestic policies are ordinarily considered to have worked if specified things do happen. Another specific example of the difference between military and domestic systems lies in the definition of waste. The criteria applied to military systems, particularly in wartime, define very little as waste unless it comes very close to outright graft and corruption; a tank or an airplane with far less utility than had been planned for, or far greater cost, has seldom been considered wasteful. One specific case of this different criterion of waste is the idea of redundancy. Military and space hardware systems are protected against failure by putting in each crucial component several times, one as backup to the other. This strong hedge against failure is applied to soft military strategy as much as it is to hardware, but politically it is almost impossible to apply to a social strategy.

In fact, when military management and planning begin to veer from the technical and tactical toward the social, even the military concept of waste and the idea of redundancy do not work too well. Military social planning is no more effective than domestic social planning, Vietnam being a case in point here.

In any case, the evidence from both domestic and military systems is clearly consistent with the theory that highly administered and planned systems fail with a high probability. What kind of systems do work under what circumstances is far less clear. Increasingly during recent years, economists, following in the wake of Milton Friedman's Chicago school, have become disillusioned with the workings of bureaucratic planning and management. And, being economists, they have turned to the market system that characterizes our American economy for the answer to many problems. This successful market system, then, provides a baseline case for the evidence in Chapter 3. The market business system of the U.S. economy contrasts with a highly administered system because it (1) is decentralized; (2) is self-administered in the sense that most of the prime actors make their own decisions; (3) is motivated by the economic self-interest of these prime actors; (4) requires only the gross application of public policy rather than detailed case-by-case application; (5) is unplanned in the sense of being laid out in advance by external authority. And the result seems to be a smoothly working economic system that is efficient in its own terms of getting maximum production from the set of resources available to the economy.

The smoothness and efficiency of the market economy does provide a very attractive model for emulation by other American subsystems. Yet it should be very clear that the economy unaided does not work well toward every social objective. For one thing, the market system does not work in regard to certain factors external to the system. Because the costs of industrial pollution have not been borne by polluting industries, for example, pollution has not been considered a cost of production like wages. The answer may lie in internalizing pollution costs, but this has not yet been done on any significant scale. And the market system has left other social problems in its wake. For instance, the economy does not always seem able to avoid severe fluctuations leading to recession and inflation or in extreme cases depression and hyperinflation. And perhaps even more important over the long run, the workings of the economy still raise important problems of distributive equity which do not seem to be answerable within the market system.

It is therefore useful to depart from the baseline case to look at other subsystems. The next case discussed is the system that attempts to improve on the unconstrained workings of the economy by controlling the business cycle. The fiscal and monetary policies of the federal government attempt to work through the market system by adjusting some of the inputs to this system without changing its attractive features of decentralization, self-administration, self-interest motivation, and the gross rather than detailed application of public policy. But though cycle control works relatively well, it does not work perfectly. While curing one of the defects of the market economy it raises its own issues. One of these is the unemployment-inflation dilemma; it has not proved possible to achieve a long-run equilibrium that combines satisfactorily low levels of unemployment with satisfactorily low rates of price increase. To solve the dilemma, attempts have occasionally been made to supplement general fiscal and monetary policy with direct price and wage controls or pseudocontrols, such as the guidelines of the mid-1960s. These controls are highly administered: They are centrally established; laid down on business and wage earners by officials acting in the public interest rather than their own self-interest; and applied in detail case by case. And they ordinarily work very badly. Similarly with the highly planned attempts to use fiscal-monetary tools in detail to fine tune cyclical policy; the attempt to hit a set level of unemployment and price increase also seems to work very badly.

The countercyclical system attempts to correct one of the flaws in the market system. The major effort to correct the other basic flaw, that of inequitable income distribution, is based on the federal income tax, the next case discussed. The federal income tax is, like the market economy and fiscal-monetary policy, not highly administered: It is decentralized and self-administered, at least in its initial application by the taxpayer to himself, and insofar as the public authorities are concerned, the federal income tax is applied grossly rather than case by case. Its self-application by the taxpayer is motivated at least in part by the negative self-interest of not being caught out. And in general, the tax system has been acceptable to the payers; there has been in the United States no large-scale tax revolt. And, with most of its characteristics resembling those of other workable systems, the federal income tax seems to work smoothly and well. At least it does insofar as it follows the above description of a low-administration system. In fact, however, there are two federal income taxes: the one described so far is that paid by most low and moderate income taxpayers whose major income comes from wage earnings. Imposed on this, however, is a far more complex system of clauses and exceptions that apply mainly to higher income earners with major income sources other than wages. This "second tax" is much more highly administered, and it works less smoothly, sometimes tending to throw the whole income tax system into doubt.

At least the federal income tax as a whole works better than the property tax which provides most local and much state revenue. The property tax is quite a different sort of system: rather than being self-administered, it is administered to taxpayers by tax assessors; rather than being motivated by self-interest, the assessors act or are supposed to act in the public interest; rather than being administered as a general policy, the property tax is administered as a set of highly specific individual assessment decisions concerning specific parcels of property and their owners. And the property tax generally works very badly indeed; it is neither efficient nor equitable. Yet the property tax does share one feature of the more successful systems discussed above, and it is one of the most frequently talked about features, decentralization. The property tax is a local tax applied by local tax authorities, about as decentralized as a public system can get. Decentralization is clearly not a sufficient condition for its success, and this throws in doubt the rush toward such decentralization advocated by some opponents of big federal government. The decentralized market system works in large measure because the decentralized decision-making units are tied together by the self-interest incentive of profit-making, and the absence of this motivation (or any other known incentive structure) from decentralized public systems is a crucial difference from the market economy.

Indeed, the next cases of similarly decentralized systems which are, like the property tax, externally rather than self-administered, administered in detail rather than as general policy, and administered in the name of the public interest rather than self-interest, provide confirming evidence of the insufficiency of decentralization without incentives. The military draft, the public assistance/welfare systems of the United States, the federal-state-local educational and manpower training systems, are all decentralized but highly administered. And they all work badly both in the sense of smooth efficiency and in the sense of equity. The above systems, however, though highly administered, do not involve comprehensive planning of varied activities toward varied objectives.

The next cases taken up concern subsystems that combine the high degree of administration of the previous ones with attempts at such comprehensive planning. Three cases are cited: the National Industrial Recovery Act of the early New Deal, the War Production Board of the Second World War, and the urban renewal effort of the 1950s and 1960s. NRA was created under the planning ethos; in fact, it provides an example of an attempt at business cartelization which never reached the stage of any real attempt at planning. NRA also illustrates the strength of self-interest, as the individual interests of the businessmen involved overwhelmed both the desire to plan and the collective interest in cartelization. WPB, however, did plan comprehensively, with the plans executed in great detail. By the testimony of those who participated, it worked poorly in the implementation of its plans. And urban renewal has proven perverse in terms of its stated goals and the reasonable expectations of its planners. Urban renewal is particularly interesting because in a sense it does use the market system to try to reach its goals, but it uses the market system and market incentives carelessly, and by so doing promotes objectives other than the ones it hopes to reach. So we can now add to decentralization as an insufficient reason for success, the use of business itself (NRA) and the use of the market system (urban renewal) as also being insufficient.

Indeed, at this point, the prognosis for public policy and planning in the future does not look good. Detailed planning and highly managed administration have not worked well, a conclusion based on the military evidence of Chapter 4 as well as the domestic evidence of Chapter 3. The market and market-like systems work, but they do not work for every public objective. They have not worked well in the area of pollution, although this may be curable within the market system; they do not work well toward distributive equity, which may be more difficult to change within the marketplace itself. Equity being basic to many of the public issues of the 1970s, this last fact becomes quite important, and the prognosis for successful pursuit of major policy objectives quite dismal.

We are not quite lost yet, however. One type of system may provide part of the answer to equity. This is a system which, like the market system, is decentralized, self-administered, motivated by self-interest incentives, and requires only gross applications of public policy rather than detailed decision-making. But it differs from the market system in that it works politically through bargaining rather than economically through the price and profit mechanism. Chapter 3 concludes with two cases of such systems: labor relations in the United States since the Wagner Act of 1935 and Community Action since the Economic Opportunity Act of 1964. Both of these have worked well as bargaining-political systems, and have changed the balance of equity in the direction desired by the designers of the systems. They do seem to provide for at least a partial rounding off of future policy systems. This is not to take the early Galbraithian point of view that countervailing power is created automatically or naturally out of the workings of our institutions. It is to say that it is possible to deliberately create such countervailing bargaining power by use of public policy.

All those systems currently in being certainly add up to a less than perfect whole. The evidence of the two chapters does suggest, however, that the beginnings of a way out of some of our current dilemmas lie in market-like and bargaining systems that combine the workable features of decentralization, self-administration, personal economic or political motivation, and the gross application of public policy rather than systems administered in detail by public officials to private clienteles according to plans laid out in detail by public planners.

None of this, however, means the abolition of bureaucracy. For better or worse, bureaucracy will continue to exist in military systems, which must remain publicly controlled, in various civil systems to which none of the above devices really apply, and in those mechanisms, such as planning itself, that must remain public even though they are directing market or bargaining systems of implementation. But some of the evidence of Chapters 3 and 4 is applicable to making bureaucracy more effective, as well as to ways and means of getting around bureaucracy. Chapter 5 summarizes the results on nonpublic mechanisms; what to do with public bureaucracy is the subject matter of Chapter 6.

3

Cases in Point: Domestic

THE FIRST CHAPTER defined "planning" as the advance laying out of a program of actions and "implementation" as the carrying out of a program of actions. It was suggested, however, that planning in the United States has taken on the more restricted meaning of a formal, comprehensive, and detailed self-conscious process. And the major discussion of the chapter was of the failure of planning in the narrower definition to come to grips with the realities of the way public programs work through from conception to implementation.

This chapter goes into cases in order to begin building some concepts of what means of planning and implementation work to what ends. The cases in this chapter concern subsystems that are primarily domestic, that is, within the United States.

Nonadministered Economic Systems

The U.S. Economy: The Business and Market System

As described in elementary economic courses, the private market system for the production and distribution of goods works very well indeed. It produces at the least possible cost the precise basket of goods and services desired by those consuming these goods and services. Every economic man pursues his own enlightened self-interest as consumer and producer, and the whole produces the most goods in the most desired mixture at the least cost. In the short run, the output of each producer is that output at which the cost of producing one more unit would exceed the price he could get for that unit, so the additional unit would be unprofitable. This means that the cost to the consumer of that good is at a minimum because nobody is making any excess profit over his cost of production (which includes a normal profit). The long run is even better because the price is determined not merely by production costs but by minimum production costs, as each producing plant ends up at a size where its average unit costs are lowest and low-cost techniques and plants drive out high-cost ones.

The motivating mechanism in this wonderful system is enlightened self-interest, namely, the desire of the businessman to make the greatest possible profit, the laborer to earn the highest possible wage, and the consumer to pay the lowest possible price. In the case of business, if a profit is too high (that is, above the normal), more businessmen will come in to gain the excess profit available and competition will reduce prices to where profits are again normal. The converse is true if profits are below normal. The whole method pervades the economy as workers gravitate toward their best wage possibilities and consumers toward lowest prices. And finally, in the long-run case, the result is reproduced on a different scale as new plants are built whenever prices above minimum possible production costs mean that new plants producing at minimum costs will bring in abnormal profits for a time.

The device that allows all this to work is competition, perfect atomistic competition with enough competitors to make sure that none has the power to affect the price of his product. Rather, each competitive producer and consumer accepts the price the market provides, and the price itself is that at which the supply produced by the tiny atomized producers is precisely equal to the demand required by the atomized consumers. Decision-making is completely decentralized; no bureaucratic mechanism is required to set prices or determine outputs centrally. Each person makes his own economic decisions, and through market competition, Adam Smith's magical "invisible hand" makes the system go.

Of course, it does not really work that way, and economists spent the nineteenth century and a good part of the twentieth realizing that it did not work that way and refining their theories to bring them closer to the way it did work. Nineteenth-

century theories of monopoly and oligopoly pointed out that
with few producers making a product instead of an atomized
multitude, the incentive for a producer was no longer to keep
on producing more until the cost of making one more unit
would exceed the price he could obtain; the incentive was to
keep prices higher (which a monopolist or oligopolist could do,
unlike an atomistic producer), obtain excess profits, and restrict
production. It was possible for a single monopolistic firm to do
this, it was possible for a few firms to do it by tacit recognition
of competitors' expected moves consequent upon their own, and
further, it was possible for a few firms to restrict entry of more
firms. In the twentieth century, the theories of imperfect and
monopolistic competition added the idea that Adam Smith's
best of all possible economic worlds might not come to pass
even with many competing firms. For if products could be dif-
ferentiated from one another, either in fact (for example, one
kind of detergent really works better than another) or in ad-
vertising (for example, one kind is blue whereas the other is
merely white), then competition is no longer between precisely
identical goods, and producers of both blue and white can each
command additional profits because some people will go out of
their way to get blue, while some will stand fast behind good
old-fashioned white.

And the system more accurately described by the newer
theories would not work as well for the public good as that described in the old theories, not by the old criteria. That is, the
maintenance of the "excess" profits of monopoly, oligopoly, or
monopolistic competition was indefinitely feasible in the real
world, and the consumer no longer received goods produced at
the minimum possible cost and price. Furthermore, the system
produced a basket of goods which was distorted relative to consumer preferences; in those product lines where excess profits
were easier to maintain, production would be more restricted
relative to those lines closer to the old model of atomistic competition. So by the old efficiency criteria, the supersession of
the theory of perfect atomistic competition threw into doubt
the perfection of the public economic good by the business system the theories purported to describe.

But also during the twentieth century, economists began to argue that the atomistic system of perfect competition had not only never existed, but that if it did, it would work very poorly indeed. The Austrian (later American) economist Joseph Schumpeter in particular argued that a dynamically growing system could not only tolerate the imperfections of monopoly, oligopoly, and monopolistic competition but required them. The engine that drove economic growth was innovation, the introduction of changes in means of production and in distribution, and this engine was powered by the possibility of obtaining over the long run just those excess profits that the perfect competition model allowed only during short periods of adjustment. Thus, for example, the desire for an excess monopoly profit was what caused the railroad barons of the nineteenth century to engage in their manipulations and speculations; monopolistic profits in large measure they certainly did obtain, but the United States was covered with a net of railroads that otherwise would have been much slower coming, and the whole country gained by it. Similarly, the innovation of Henry Ford in mass-producing low-priced automobiles brought him vast profits because he sold cheaper than other people. But the country also was better off for the Model T and all the roads and industries that followed on the Model T than it would have been without Ford and his assembly line and his excess profits. (The fact that the market has produced automobiles that have produced smog will be taken up shortly.)

And the surprising thing is that even though the various monopolistic models revise drastically what the early economists thought to be essential in making the economy work for the public good, they turn out to preserve much more of the old theories (properly interpreted) and the old values than would appear obvious. Because the essential mechanism of Smith's economic theory was not the perfection of competition leading to the minimization of prices in the long and short run, but rather the invisible hand by which a wide variety of decentralized decision-makers (for example, businessmen, workers, consumers) each figured out his own self-interest, made his own decisions, and made the entire system run without being administered by any external decision-maker. All this, plus the objective test of the success of the participants in the system—the test of profits and business survival—remained in the Schumpeter as well as the Smith version of the theory. The number of decentralized decision centers on the business production side is far fewer in the modern theories, the test is not exactly the same one in the modern theories, perhaps not even the right one according to the old theories, but it is an objective test. And the parts fit together in a way not too dissimilar from that described in the old theories.

They key point is that the system works. The obsolescence of the original theory means that the system does not work to produce the minimum-price precisely correct basket of goods that was the key philosophical and political argument for the Smith system, but it works. In the first instance, it works primarily in just working; that is, goods and services are produced and income provided to the producers smoothly. The importance of just plain smoothness is difficult to exaggerate; the ease with which this decentralized self-interest motivated system moves as compared to the harsh gratings of centralized unmotivated administrative systems, some of which are described below, may be its chief attraction.

But the attractiveness goes far beyond just smooth working. The economy not only works, but in the United States it grows at a satisfactory rate. Ignoring for the moment the business cycle, over the long run the American economy produces more each year than it had the year before. Furthermore, the pattern of production of goods and services is at least similar to the desired pattern, that is, the pattern desired by consumers with money to spend, and it adapts quickly to changes in the pattern. (The equity of the pattern of spending capability—income—will be taken up shortly.)

We cannot say, of course, that the market system as it exists in the United States is the best possibly available, measured against the criteria of growth, of fulfilling consumer desires, of production at lowest costs, or of smooth operation. We cannot even say that it is necessarily the best economic system around; the situations of different countries using different systems depend on too many variables to make any precise comparisons meaningful. The economy of the United States is clearly in far better working order than that of any Latin American country, but not only is the production-distribution system different, so also are the resource endowments, the climates, and the populations; it is impossible to say definitively what are the primary causal factors in our advantage. But some rough comparisons are possible among countries in similar situations. The United States, Germany, and Japan, with decentralized market-oriented economic systems (decentralized in each case, even though Germany and Japan are substantially more oligopolistic than the United States), seem to have far better working economies than the centralized Soviet Union, in spite of the fact that the Soviet Union is highly endowed with resources and a technologically capable population. The free German economy works better than that planned by the Nazis, the West German economy better than the planned East German.

In any case, the argument that the business system described by the old and new theories is the best possible is specious; the argument that it is the best around is stronger but not demonstrable. The really strong argument is merely that this is a very workable system. But even this very workable system is by no means good or even acceptable on all the possible criteria for an economic system. It is smooth, it grows, its pattern of production is in rough accord with consumer desire, and so forth. But on at least three very important counts, the business system taken by itself has worked very poorly.

1. It takes into account only those factors that are included within the market. The theory is that the business firm buys factors of production, such as labor time, capital equipment, and materials, on the market and that if the prices of these factors are high, the firm will charge high prices, sell less than at lower prices, and buy fewer factors. This works reasonably well for those factors that are bought on the market, but such factors as air are not bought, nor is the right to create such public nuisances as noise or water pollution. (Water, as such, is bought, but the right to discharge effluents has generally been free or subject only to small sewer charges.) And because these "exter-

nal" factors of production do not enter the cost of production to the firm at anywhere near the levels at which they form real costs to the health and comfort of the population, nuisance-causing production and the dangers it brings are much greater than they would be if the product were sold at prices that reflected the "external" costs. The importance of these factors external to the market has increased rapidly in the public eye (or, in the case of air pollution, the public eyes) during recent years, though the economic theory of externalities has been around for some time. The description of pollution and allied problems in economic terms does carry with it the seeds of one possible solution, namely, through tax and similar devices to make sure that the "external" costs to the public are also "internal" costs to the producing companies; but this solution (or any other) has been implemented only meagerly, and externally caused problems of this nature must be currently counted as failures of the market system.

2. A second failure of the business system to work, unaided, for the general good lies in the fact that in the past, at least, it has worked unevenly over time. Through the 1930s, the business system of the United States and the rest of the world was frequently plagued by massive depression with all the consequent reductions of production, unemployment, and real human suffering. From the 1930s through the 1950s, fluctuations were small but still existed. During the 1960s it began to look as if perhaps fluctuations were correctable, but the relevant point here is that they were not automatically corrected by the decentralized decision-making of the business system in the same way in which long-run economic growth and smooth operation stemmed from the automatic workings of decentralization. The business cycle appears curable without making major changes in the business system, but the cure is outside the system itself. In the midst of the Great Depression of the 1930s, economic theories of "secular stagnation" held that the business system itself was breaking down, that not merely was the business cycle with its depressions and inflations inevitable, but the long-run economic growth that was the business system's chief attraction had ceased. Had this been true, the business system could have

been said to have failed. Since it turned out not to be true, the system has not failed on that count, and since the business cycle seems curable or ameliorable from outside the business system, the system's failure to solve the cycle is not an overwhelming criticism. But the point is that in using the business system as an example of a success, it should be clear that the system taken alone has not been an unmixed success; through the 1930s it caused great human misery in depressions.

3. The other drawback of the business system is not so easily remedied, even from outside the system. The business system does not provide equitable distribution of income, or at least not a distribution that is equitable according to modern values. The income-distribution criterion implicit in the work of most nineteenth-century capitalist economists was not that characterized by Marx as "from each according to his abilities, to each according to his needs." Rather, the criterion would distribute income to each according to his contribution to the economy, and the business system might be said to satisfy this criterion by definition. The argument would be that the only way to measure objectively an individual's contribution to the economy is by the payment he receives for this contribution, and by this definition, he is paid according to his contribution —a pure tautology. Beyond tautology, the point made by Schumpeter was that the monopoly profits, which are a major cause of unequal income distribution, are justified by the contributions of the entrepreneurs whose innovations are what makes the economy grow so rapidly. In fact, normative analysis of income distribution has never been satisfactorily handled by economists. The best they have been able to do is the "Pareto optimum," which essentially ignores the problem, saying that an improvement to one man's income is fine if it does not reduce another man's, and thus takes the original distribution as given.

In any case, modern value systems have shifted in some measure toward the Marxian "from each according to his abilities, to each according to his needs." And the modern business system is not necessarily at all equitable according to the needs criterion. The income distribution of the United States and other business countries may or may not be inequitable; it is certainly unequal, and in the judgment of many people, so unequal as to be inequitable. Furthermore, there is near consensus in the United States that at least at the bottom of the scale of income distribution there is real inequity to the extent that some people are allowed to starve and suffer from extreme poverty in a very wealthy system. And in addition to the questions about distribution of income as such, questions are increasingly raised about the distribution of political power which to a large extent goes with the distribution of income. On these counts of equality and equity, the business system does not work well. And unlike the case of the business cycle, the necessary external corrections to the system are by no means obvious.

To sum up this discussion of the basic U.S. economic system: The business-market system works very well by many criteria; it is by no means perfect because by certain very important criteria it works rather poorly. Some of these misfunctionings are correctable in part by other subsystems in the overall American system; some may be more difficult to correct. But on the other hand, it may well be that the elements of decentralization and utilization of self-interest that power the best as well as the worst parts of the business system are applicable to other subsystems in the United States which at this time work much more poorly than the private economy.

The Business Cycle: Fiscal and Monetary Policy

It was suggested above that one major fault in the uncorrected business system is its tendency toward cyclical fluctuation. This now seems in large measure to be correctable without major changes within the business system itself. That is, the depression-inflation business cycle seems avoidable, or at least meliorable in a major way without changing the key decentralization and self-interest motivation features of the business system. Rather, the correction can be made by using the central decision-making authority of the government to change the factors affecting the self-interest by which decentralized business decision-makers work. This can be done without changing the decentralization itself.

In a highly simplified description, the primary cause of the business cycle lies in the decisions of private investors in business plant and equipment, or of the government itself, to increase or decrease purchases of the goods private investors and the government purchase. (Consumers' decisions to increase or decrease purchases have been generally considered consequent upon other decisions and therefore not first-order causes of the cycle.) The change in the investors' and the government's demand in turn changes the profits of those who sell to them, and the sellers' consequent decisions to produce less or more, employ fewer or more, raise or lower prices, or whatever, have chain effects on those who sell to sellers. The original decisions thus expand mightily through the so-called multiplier mechanism. The multiplier works through employees and other suppliers who sell their services to employers and who, when the sales of their services vary, in turn vary their purchases, and so on through the chain. It is still a somewhat open question in economic theory as to whether these changes in consumer and similar purchases in turn react back on the plant and equipment investment decisions that may have begun the whole chain. The accelerator theory, less well-established or specified than the multiplier theory, has it that plant and equipment expenditures depend in turn on the predicted sales of the consumer goods to be produced by the plant and equipment and that this series of consumer-producer-investor actions and reactions generates the whole business cycle.

The validity of the accelerator theory is not important here, however, because it is clear that though cycle-generating variations in private investment may be dependent on the cycle itself, cycle-generating variations in government expenditures and revenues can be deliberately manipulated by policy and thus can be used by central decision-making authority to change the cycle. If consumer and investor demand for goods and services is too high, thus causing inflationary pressure, the government can compensate; similarly, if it is too low. Whether the compensation is through fiscal policy or monetary policy is also relatively unimportant here. By the use of fiscal policy, the government compensates directly by spending more or less to make up for the rest of the economy spending less or more, or the government compensates indirectly by raising or lowering taxes, thus encouraging the rest of the economy to spend less or more. Monetary policy is also indirect because government regulation of the availability of money and the level of interest rates works via encouraging more or less private spending. There are important differences among variation of government spending, variation of taxes, and variation of money supply; such variations in particular can change the mix of things produced and the distribution of income. But the point here is that through any of these devices or a combination of these devices, the government can go a long way in effectively smoothing out the business cycle and can do this without substituting public administration for the power of decentralized producers and consumers to make their own decisions on what they perceive to be their own best interests.

Again, however, government compensatory policy is workable, as is the business system as a whole, but it does not solve all problems, as the business system does not. It was a very long and difficult political sales job indeed to establish the government in the compensatory policy field, particularly compensatory fiscal policy. During the late 1940s, many advocates of compensatory fiscal policy, such as Professor Alvin Hansen of Harvard, despaired of having their ideas adopted. During the Eisenhower years, in the 1950s, the concepts began to be utilized sub rosa without the administration admitting that it was compensating, and against the will of some of its members, such as Secretary of the Treasury George Humphrey. Not until the Kennedy administration did the government admit that it was in fact trying to compensate; the key events were President Kennedy's speech at Yale University in June 1962 advocating compensatory policy and his 1963 proposal for a tax cut in spite of the large government deficit, which proposal was later carried through by President Johnson.

But in the long process of selling compensatory fiscal policy, it was in a sense oversold. It was made to look too simple. At least one important problem of the business cycle has not yet proven solvable within either the business system or the federal compensatory system that goes with the business system. This is the relationship between the level of aggregate economic activity, as represented particularly by employment, and the level of prices. Positive government compensatory action to increase the level of activity increases employment and reduces unemployment; in many cases it also raises prices. Negative action to reduce or level off prices may also level off employment and increase unemployment. The reason for this lies in the very decentralization of the business system. Given increased demands for their products, businessmen can produce more or raise their prices, or both. And though we would like them to respond to positive government compensatory action by increasing production and employment and to negative action by holding or reducing prices, businessmen just do not respond that way. If more profit can be made by increasing prices than by increasing production, it will be done; and indeed the decentralized self-interest ethos of the business system says it should be done, for once business starts acting in other than its own self-interest, the system begins to break down. Labor, particularly organized labor, is a bit tougher to fit into the model of decentralized self-interest, because collectively bargained wage rates are not ordinarily constrained by the quantity of labor a trade union wishes to sell in the same way prices are constrained by the quantity of goods a firm wishes to sell. Unions just do not bargain that way, and thus their pressure is always for higher wages. At least, this is the way many businessmen tend to think of unions; in fact, the distinction is fuzzy, and equity at least would seem to suggest that if business is ethical in raising prices when it is able, labor is equally ethical in raising wages when it can.

In any case, the result of all these complex relationships among different kinds of public and private actions is that in many situations tolerable levels of unemployment (say, 3.5 percent or below) go with intolerable levels of price increase (say, 5 percent a year or above). The only way to slow down inflation thus implies raising unemployment to levels that are also intolerable.

This is an oversimplified and static explanation of a phenomenon that depends very much on time and dynamics, but the point is that it is typically difficult or impossible to match acceptable levels of unemployment with acceptable rates of price increase for long. And thus the government compensatory subsystem added on to the business subsystem still fails to find solutions for all relevant and crucial problems.

A related unsolved problem of government compensation is that of fine tuning. "Fine tuning" is that process by which those who direct government compensatory policy try to pick the best possible combination of employment and price increase and to hit that precise point. This involves not merely the level of compensation but the mixture and timing of compensatory policy—government spending, taxation, and monetary policy—and indeed substantial detail within each of these types of policy. Particular bottlenecks make a difference; upward pressure on the housing market, for example, may cause housing prices and rents to increase, and this may in turn cause more pressure on wages.

The attempt to fine tune compensatory policy has not worked well. For one thing, it cannot allow for lags in institutional responses to policy with any precision; neither output nor price responses are immediate, and some are very slow, popping up after they are expected or wanted. These lags, in turn, can lead to overkill if a slow-acting effort to move the economy in a desired direction causes the government compensators to put on more and more pressure until the economy does turn around and move in the opposite direction too far too fast. What it comes to is that the science of economics is well enough developed to predict statistically the overall trends in a decentralized system, but still has substantial difficulty in predicting turning points from one trend to another. Turning points are based on relationships like ratios, where a small move in the numerator or denominator may mean a very large move in the ratio itself.

And beyond the inability of economists to predict very precisely the turning points in the private economy, it is at least as difficult to have the precisely desired effect on the public decision process. Lags here, too, tend to defeat fine tuning. In the

case of the inflation of the late 1960s, the price rises were predictable enough that economists generally agreed that the administration should have asked for a compensatory tax increase
earlier than it did in 1967. Unfortunately, President Johnson
did not agree, Congress took its time, and the tax increase was
not passed until 1968. The U.S. Congress is one of the few legislative bodies in the world with real control over taxes and
spending. In any case, the net result in 1968 was a failure of
the desired fine tuning effect in slowing down the inflation as
soon or as much as had been hoped for.

Another attempt to solve some of the unemployment-inflation contradictions of compensatory federal policy was the so-
called guidelines policy of the early and mid-1960s. The idea
was for the government to set guidelines on price and wage increases that, if adhered to by business and labor, would keep
the increases down to what the traffic would bear. The guidelines worked, in part and for a while, but their effect was only
transitory. Two types of guidelines were attempted: (1) The first
set a general rule—unenforced except by moral suasion—that
prices should not increase except to cover cost increases, and
wages should not increase more than the average annual increase in labor productivity of 3–5 percent. If wage increases
were kept to these levels, on the average business costs would
not increase; wage increases would be compensated for by the
greater productivity of wage earners. Those firms and industries
with greater than average productivity increases would thus
have falling average costs and should reduce prices; those increasing productivity less than average would have rising average costs and would be allowed to raise prices. But average
price levels would remain constant. (2) Attempts were made to
impose guidelines in specific cases, such as steel, where crucial
price and wage decisions were being made, and where public
visibility and potential government activity in such areas as antitrust and federal procurement meant that the suasion was
something more than moral.

The difficulty with the guidelines policy was that it interfered
with the very basis of the business system, the decentralized
self-interest–guided method of decision-making. The specific

applications to such industries as steel meant the imposition of central authority—moral or otherwise—on these industries. And even the general policy meant the substitution of a centrally determined numerical rule as a guideline instead of a self-interested desire to maximize income. A numerical rule might have worked if everyone had accepted the rule of a given percentage as a substitute for self-interest in guiding their own decisions. But neither business nor labor did; nor were they likely to. Self-interest is easy to rationalize; any percentage rule is too easy to call unfair to oneself and overly fair to someone else. And the abandonment of self-interest seems to lead to self-pity, which in turn leads to self-justification in breaking the rules.

Wage and price control through guidelines and suasion thus worked imperfectly. And as for legal as compared to moral price and wage control, this is an alternative to compensatory policy that is unlikely to work for long. It should be possible in principle to assure very full employment through strong positive federal compensatory policy and to prevent inflation by slapping legal ceilings on prices and wages. If this were attempted over any lengthy time period, a necessary concomitant would be rationing, since controlled prices and wages fail to perform the function of allocating productive resources among goods to produce the desired market basket.

Before 1971, there had been two major periods of price control in the United States, the World War II period from 1942 to 1946 and the Korean War period from 1950 to 1953. Price and wage controls and rationing did undoubtedly keep prices during these two periods below what they would have been without controls. In principle, of course, it would have been possible to achieve the same or even a greater degree of stability by retaining a decentralized price system and using a countercyclical policy to combat inflation; in practice it was neither politically possible, nor could it have been equitable.

The problem, particularly in World War II, was that if a free price-wage system were used to allocate productive resources to those uses that the tasks of war demanded, a new and elaborate system of price and wage incentives would have had to be created within the system. The government would have had to bid high enough to get producers of automobiles to turn to tanks, and tank producers would have had to bid for steel and for labor. Effective demand for such war goods and resources would have shot up, and to prevent hyperinflation, total demand would have had to be kept in line by reducing demand elsewhere through extremely heavy taxes. On grounds of equity, these taxes would have had to fall heavily on everybody. Yet this would have introduced a major dilemma: Heavy taxes falling on those whom the new incentive structure was supposed to induce to change their economic activities would have decreased incentive-producing wages and profits to the point where the incentives were ineffective. Conceptually, this would have been the problem; in practical terms it would have been exacerbated even further by real reductions of supply in some goods, such as coffee and sugar. (For others, such as meat and butter, the shortage problem was one less of supply than of increased demand by a population that could afford good meat and butter for the first time since the Depression.) And politically, it would have been impossible to impose such heavy taxes, particularly if they were inequitable and incentive-preserving.

In any case, price and wage controls and rationing were substituted for such a hypothetical price system, and to some degree they worked. But they worked at the cost of great inefficiency, particularly in the consumer sector, inefficiency both in the sense of misallocating goods produced relative to consumer desires and of producing these goods more expensively than was necessary because productive resources too were misallocated. Controls worked at the cost of undoubted inequities, and some degree of crime and black-market corruption. The reaction of this even now has been summarized well by President Nixon. When Secretary of the Treasury David Kennedy hinted during mid-1969 that wage and price controls might be necessary to contain inflation, the hint was rather obviously a form of pressure on the Congress not to reduce taxes. Even so, the effect on the President himself seems to have been rather traumatic, as reported by *The New York Times.*

The President, it is understood, responded in terms something like the following:

Controls! O, my God, no! I was a lawyer in O.P.A. [Office of Price Administration] during the war and I know all about controls. They mean rationing, black markets, inequitable administration. We'll never go for controls.[1]

It seems likely that the President expressed the common view. Indeed, after World War II, in 1946, President Truman found it absolutely impossible to continue with price control and rationing in order to contain inflation. The moral imperative of winning the war being gone, the system simply broke down.

Nonetheless, because of a deteriorating national and international economic situation in 1971, President Nixon introduced peacetime price and wage controls, countering his own previously expressed objections by making them temporary and selective, and enforcing them primarily by moral suasion, rather than a new OPA. Predictably, they worked selectively and temporarily at best (though the once-for-all effect of the initial freeze may have been important as a break in long-run inflationary expectations).

At any rate, as in the case of the business system as a whole, business-cycle compensatory federal policy works, but not for everything. Its workings are limited by the unemployment-inflation relationship, and to this problem no answer has been found within either the business system or the compensatory system. And answers outside the system, such as price and wage controls, whether moral or legal, have worked badly and temporarily, and, after a time, not at all.

The Federal Individual Income Tax

In the discussion of the workings of the business-market economy of the United States, three important exceptions were noted to the general workability attributed to the system. The system itself can give powerful assistance in correcting one of these, environmental pollution, though this has not yet been done to any significant degree. Attempts to correct the second of the faults, the business system's tendency to generate a depression-inflation business cycle if uncontrolled, have been discussed in the previous section. The third flaw, however, the fact that the uncontrolled system creates an income distribution that is inequitable by modern standards, is more intractable than the other two.

One major attempt to deal with income distribution in the United States has been through the tax system. The federal individual income tax, in particular, is in theory at least designed in large part to meliorate income inequity by taxing high incomes more heavily than low. A thoroughgoing analysis of the effect of taxes on income distribution would necessarily be concerned with the entire tax system, not only the individual income tax but all federal taxes and indeed the entire federal-state-local system of taxes paid by people and transfer payments to people, since the income an individual can spend on his own needs is the remainder left over after paying all taxes, augmented by payments (such as old age pensions under Social Security) he gets from government. Since the focus here is on administration rather than substance, however, parts of the system can be singled out for special examination. The federal income tax, standing by itself, provides an example of one kind of public system which may be contrasted administratively with other kinds, particularly state and local property tax systems.

Three sorts of measures may be applied to the evaluation of a tax: the revenue it brings in, its effects on the economy within which it operates, and its effects on distributive equity. The evaluation of equity in turn must be approached from the standpoint of two criteria: the way the tax treats people with different incomes and the way it treats people in similar economic circumstances. A good tax will not only treat people with different income levels differently (the equity criterion for income distribution discussed above) but it will also treat people with the same income the same.

These three economic criteria—revenue, economic effects, and equity—all bear heavily on a final administrative consideration on which the workability of the tax depends. This is its acceptability to the taxpayers. Acceptability is crucial because no tax system can work by rigid enforcement alone; were all payments forced out of the taxpayer, the system would not only be unworkable in a free society but the cost of enforcement would in itself consume a good portion of the tax revenue.

The ideal model of the individual income tax is one in which the taxpayers understand the rules and are willing to follow them with a minimum of coercion, in which the tax is assessed by the payers themselves on the basis of their own incomes. In the ideal model, enforcement is by exception. That is, it is assumed that taxpayers have assessed themselves fairly and correctly, and the only time the enforcement apparatus enters in is when the opposite is discovered. This contrasts to a system where the assumption is that the taxpayer will cheat unless an official is looking over his shoulder at all times. In this ideal model, the exception system is in turn generally applied by auditing a sample of returns; a small chance that he will be caught out is sufficient to keep the taxpayer on the straight and narrow. Both self-administration and enforcement are aided by tax withholding. Thus, this simplified and ideal model resembles the models of the working of the overall economy and of the business cycle control apparatus in that the individual within the system makes decisions for himself. Unlike the two previous cases, the individual does not make his decisions in his own self-interest, which presumably would be to not pay taxes, but in a general willingness to conform with a public interest that is clearly delineated by the laws and rules of the tax system. The willingness is bolstered by fear and sample enforcement as well as by habit, but the system is far different from one in which every tax return is computed centrally.

The ideal model of the federal individual income tax, then, is acceptable to the taxpayer by definition. It also rates high marks on the other criteria of a good tax. (1) The revenue from the tax can be expanded or contracted within wide limits by simple variation of the tax rates. (2) In its economic effects, the ideal income tax is quite close to being neutral with regard to matters on which tax neutrality is generally considered preferable, particularly to matters of allocation of economic resources. Whereas other taxes tend to bias the allocation of resources according to consumer desires which is considered a chief advan-

tage of the market economy, the individual income tax intro-
duces such biases seldom or not at all. A sales tax, for
example, will raise the prices of the goods taxed, as compared
to other goods and thus decrease the resources devoted to producing the taxed goods, compared to what the consumers would
demand in a free market. Even a general sales tax on all goods
will introduce a bias by making saving more attractive relative
to consumer expenditure than it otherwise would have been.
An ideal property tax—on land alone but not buildings or
other improvements—shares the attractive economic neutrality
of the income tax, because land is not produced by use of economic resources; it is just there. For this reason, Henry
George's nineteenth-century proposals for a single tax on land
alone have always been attractive to economists. In practice
today, however, property taxes cover goods, such as buildings
on the land, that use up real resources in their production, and
thus bias the market against building, just as a sales tax would.
In any case, the ideal individual income tax biases only one decision, that made by the earner between income-producing (and
therefore taxable) work effort and leisure. This decision is not
generally considered crucial to the economy, and thus the individual income tax is close to the neutral ideal. (3) The income
tax can be brought to conform with current ideas of equity
more easily than any other tax. As noted, current concepts of
equity relate largely to size of income (as compared, for example, to medieval concepts, which related more to role in life)
and size of income is of course directly affected by the individual income tax. Thus, the ideal of income equalization is expressed in the progressive rates of the federal income tax: The
receivers of incomes so low that they fall below personal exemptions and standard deductions pay no income tax; the rate
on the first dollars earned above exemptions and deductions is
only 14 percent (and the average rate on the total income of the
lower-bracket receiver is much lower because of the zero tax on
the exempted and deducted portions). And for the higher-
bracket taxpayer, the rate on marginal income goes all the way
up to 70 percent—very progressive indeed. Furthermore, the
other ideal of equity, treating likes alike, is also fulfilled by the

ideal individual income tax because likes are defined by having like income which is taxed alike.

In fact, as in the case of the market economy and business-cycle policy, the real federal individual income tax is far from identical with the ideal model. To begin with, it is really two income taxes: (1) There is a basic, simple, individual income tax, not too dissimilar from the ideal model, in which the taxpayer pays according to a simple rate schedule applied to an easily defined concept of income, earned by him in gainful employment. (2) On top of the simple tax is applied another system with a fantastically complex set of exceptions, applying in the main to a minority of taxpayers. Legally, the two systems are not separated; in actuality they are.

For the simple portion of the overall individual income tax, payment is assisted by withholding of an employee's tax by his employer and by a standard deduction, which means he can avoid figuring out the deductions he might take. Like the ideal model, this basic income tax is self-assessed (and withholding statements and standard deductions make self-assessment easier) and is enforced by exception with a rather small sample generally considered sufficient to keep the wage earner honest. Withholding not only assists the taxpayer, but also assists the enforcer.

The relative importance of this simple income tax in the whole individual income tax might be measured very conservatively by the proportion of income tax returns that claim the standard deduction rather than itemizing deductions (59 percent in 1966). But since about two-thirds of the itemized deduction returns reported only wage and salary income (the corresponding figure for standard deduction returns is seven-eighths),[2] it seems safe to say that at least three-quarters of all the taxpayers are under the simple system. (Were this primarily an economic analysis of the income tax, the relevant statistics would concern the proportions of taxable income and tax revenue covered by the simple standard deduction-withholding system, but since the study is of methods of administration, the proportion of total number of returns is the more relevant concept. Similarly, the homeowners' interest and tax deductions, which are the major ones on most of the 41 percent of returns that itemize deductions, raise important economic issues, but administratively they are quite simple for most taxpayers who itemize.)

The second portion of the individual income tax is far more complicated. It imposes on the simple idea of clearly defined income and basic rates a complex system of exceptions with various purposes. For one thing, income itself needs a much more complex definition when the costs of earning the income are brought into the picture. For the wage earner, these costs are simple and trivial: perhaps certain work equipment and not much more. But for the merchant of one variety or another, for example, it is clearly unfair to tax that portion of gross income paid out for stock in trade. And things get progressively more complex as one approaches cases such as those for which some portion of entertainment expenses is properly deducted as being necessary to earn the income taxed.

Another complexity derives from the attempt to introduce various kinds of special equity into the tax law. The political decision has been made, for example, that it is equitable to tax those with heavy medical payments less than those without; deduction of medical payments and similar deductions add many complexities. But probably the greatest set of complexities is that added by the use of the income tax law to achieve a wide variety of social purposes. Allowing deductions for charitable contributions, for example, achieves the social purpose of increasing the funds that citizens will contribute to charities and to foundations. This is clearly a noble purpose, but it becomes complex indeed with the introduction of rules concerning the deductible value of things, for example, works of art given to charities. And charity is only one of many social purposes promoted within this complex second portion of the federal individual income tax. Urban finances are promoted by making the income from municipal bonds tax free, discovery of oil resources is promoted (at least in theory) by the depletion allowance on oil income, and so forth. And under the guise of social purpose, tax equity, or fair definition of income, many very special provisions benefiting special taxpayers have been introduced into the tax law. For example, when antitrust action forced DuPont to divest itself of General Motors stock, a special legislative provision ensured that DuPont would not be taxed fully on the unwanted profit from the sale; a special provision also was once written so that it benefited movie mogul Louis B. Mayer, and Mayer alone, giving him a tax break on a complex and unique financial transaction.

One reason for the plethora of special provisions has to do with the acceptability of the individual income tax among politically potent high-income taxpayers. The progressive rates mentioned above as applying to high income are so high that they discourage earning incentives among those who have to pay them (or so it is claimed): "Who wants to make an effort to earn an extra dollar the government is going to take away?" This contention on the work-discouraging effects of high marginal taxes may be questionable; what is certain, however, is that the high marginal taxes induce strong incentives on the part of the wealthy to avoid them. And the multitude of special exceptions reduce the actual effective rates of income taxes on the rich, thus making the income tax acceptable to the rich, but do so without changing the ostensible high marginal rates that make the tax acceptable to the less well off.

In any case, this complex second portion of the individual income tax is interpreted by self-interest so as to maximize the retained income of the payers. In this sense, it is a decentralized self-interest-motivated system similar in its working to the overall economy. But the legislative setting and administrative interpretation of the rules under which this self-interest is maximized is so complex that this second portion of the individual income tax is also largely an administered system subject to considerable discretion on the part of officials acting on other individuals in behalf of what they believe to be the public good.

Because of the existence of the double individual income tax —the complex as well as the simple portion—the evaluation of the tax as it really is is a good deal less straightforward than the evaluation of the ideal model. On the first criterion, revenue, the individual income tax still rates high, though its money-raising capacity may be more limited politically than might be observed from a theoretical examination of the ideal version.

On the second criterion, its economic effects, however, the income tax as it is is substantially less neutral than the income tax as it is idealized. This is particularly the case because the economic effects of the income tax must be looked at in conjunction with the effects of other taxes collected from the same sources. To give one example, a major impact on the development or nondevelopment of cities has come from the combination of the individual income tax with the local property tax. One of the special provisions within the complex portion of the individual income tax allows property owners to depreciate the value of structures on their property very rapidly, deduct the depreciation from income (as a cost of obtaining the income earned from the property) and thus lower their income taxes. After the propertied taxpayer has depreciated the value to where none is remaining on the books, he may then sell the property to another taxpayer who can start the depreciation all over again on the basis of the price he paid the first man. The economic effect of this is to preserve old buildings, depreciate them rapidly, and spend little or nothing on maintenance—a formula for slum creation. Added to this, then, is the fact that property tax (as it is, rather than the single tax version) taxes the value of structures as well as land; since old buildings are valued lower than new buildings, there is additional incentive against new buildings—again, an incentive to retain slums. The slum-preserving economic effects of these two taxes are probably far more powerful than the slum-destroying incentives in the Urban Renewal Program. And the example shows the difficulty of planning without considering the effects of special incentives.

If the revenue-raising effects of the two-phase income tax are still pretty good and the economic effects far less neutral than in the idealized version, the effects of the tax as it really exists on equity are mixed. Considering first the kind of equity that treats people within the same income groups similarly, the simple version of the tax, applying mainly to earners of lower incomes, works pretty well. With certain exceptions (for example, homeowners and married people being able to split income and thus pay substantially lower rates on the progressive scale than single people) wage earners with standard or simple deductions pay about the same as other wage earners at the same income level. For the higher, more complex portion of the income tax, however, this within-income-class equity is more questionable. Those who have oil income, income from municipal bonds, capital gains, and the like pay lower taxes than those whose similar command of economic resources stems from higher salaries. These differences can be overstated; when people get into income brackets where variations of this sort make a big difference, they tend to manage their affairs so that they will receive the advantages of the variations, for example, business executives being compensated by stock options on which they pay lower capital gains taxes rather than by salaries on which the taxes are higher or movie stars owning ranches. But even so, substantial differences do exist within the higher income classes affected by the complex version of the tax.

And the special provisions that bring about this spotty equity within income classes also affect the equity of the income tax (the overall income tax with both parts put together) as among different income classes. On the average, the income tax as it exists is still progressive, though not so progressive as would be assumed from the high and rapidly increasing rates discussed above. Joseph Pechman estimates, for example, that under the 1964 tax law, the nominal average tax rates for annual incomes in the $9,000–$10,000, $25,000–$50,000, and $1 million brackets were 22 percent, 39 percent, and 69 percent, respectively, but the actual effective rates in the same brackets after personal exemptions, deductions, capital gains provisions, and income splitting for married couples were 10 percent, 19 percent, and 27 percent, respectively.[3] Thus, though the tax is still progressive (19 percent for rich people and 27 percent for millionaires is a good deal higher than the 10 percent effective rate in the $9,000–$10,000 category), it is far less effective in equalizing incomes than would be implied by the ostensible 39 percent rate for the wealthy and 69 percent for millionaires, as compared to the 22 percent rate in the lower bracket.

And if the average tax rate is still progressive, the average is not the only statistic to be looked at. Those special provisions that make the burdens within high income groups unequal are for various social reasons probably acceptable within these income groups; at least one seldom hears an automobile executive complaining about the depletion allowance available to an oil millionaire, probably because of the equalizing effect available to the auto man from buying oil stock, among other things. But these inequities within the group also become specific cases in inequity among groups, as in the cases of the millionaires who pay no taxes because their income is from tax-free municipal bonds and the oil men who pay relatively little. These are well known and are tough to take on the part of those who are subject to the simple variety of income tax, have their wages withheld at the source, and pay out a good fraction of their small incomes to the federal government. And all this, in turn, affects the acceptability of the individual income tax. As noted above, the special provisions help make the ostensibly highly progressive rates of the tax acceptable to the well off. On the other hand, the well-publicized exceptions make it less acceptable to those who routinely pay taxes in the simple portion of the system. This problem is probably solvable by the kind of tax reforms that cut down both on the special provisions and the ostensibly high rates, but this can only be done through a difficult political process made more difficult by the fact that though there is little lobbying for special provisions in general, each separate provision has its vociferous and powerful backers. Attempts at such reforms were made in the Congress in 1969; they were not successful.

In any case, the individual income tax as it really exists occasionally comes close to a crisis of acceptability. And as noted above, acceptability is very important, since in a decentralized self-applied system, modified by a willingness to bow to the public interest rather than self-interest, nonacceptability means a failure to work. For this reason, the income tax does not work in many underdeveloped nations. Even in as modern a country as France, the income tax system came near to breaking down during the 1950s when the small-business taxpayers led by Pierre Poujade revolted against the multitude of special provisions that seemed especially burdensome to the small shopkeeper but not the big businessman.

The federal individual income tax in the United States, however, is ordinarily still well within the bounds of acceptability, and it may become more so as it is amended to bring the ostensible rates nearer to the real ones. And as long as it remains acceptable, any evaluation of it must sum up heavily on the favorable side. It is a good revenue producer, its economic effects, though far from neutral, are more neutral than those of many other taxes, and it is reasonably equitable both within and among income classes. It has defects, but many of them are curable within the system. And, finally, and more important in a study of the administration of public programs, it works smoothly; that in itself is a major consideration.

Administered Systems

The State and Local Property Tax

The property tax, which provides a major portion of the revenues of states and localities (about one-third in 1962), is generally considered far less acceptable than either federal or state income taxes. Tax protests in general are, of course, widespread; no one really likes to have money taken away from him without being given specific goods or services in return. But protests about taxes most frequently concern the overall level of these taxes, and in the case of income taxes in particular, it is the rates and some features of the structure (particularly the structure of the more complex portion of the income tax) that engender political trouble. Except for some segments of the far, far right, however, the income tax as such is not questioned.

In the case of property taxes, protests are frequently and very specifically levied against the form of the tax. In California, for example, a referendum passed in November 1968 provided property tax relief even though it was known that alternative sources of funds would have to be found within the state income and sales taxes. The passage of the California referendum precluded passage of an even harsher referendum, which would have put a rigid ceiling on property taxes. And still, in a survey taken in August 1970, the property tax rated as by far the most unpopular of state levies, more than twice as unpopular as its nearest competitor, the state income tax.

Why? There are numerous specific complaints about the property tax, but many stem from the fact that the property tax, unlike the income tax, is administered to the taxpayers by people other than themselves. The property tax is assessed; someone else makes a decision as to the value of your property and, subject to a frequently difficult appeals procedure, the assessor's judgment determines the tax you pay. The specific difficulties with assessment are numerous and will be discussed below, but these difficulties, which resemble the problems with defining equity in the complex portion of the income tax, would be far less irritating if the property tax could be self-assessed, as is even the complex portion of the income tax.

The property tax has long been the subject of severe criticism. Henry George's tax proposals to apply the property tax only to land values were made during the 1880s when property taxes of the current sort—taxing land, structures, and other improvements—provided the great bulk of governmental revenue in the United States and were already unpopular.

In 1931, Jens Jensen wrote:

If any tax could have been eliminated by adverse criticism, the general property tax should have been eliminated long ago. One searches in vain for one of its friends to defend it intelligently. It is even difficult to find anyone who has given it careful study who can subsequently speak of its failure in temperate language. . . . Should some prosecuting attorney drag the tax as a culprit before a bar of justice, he would be embarrassed by the abundance of expert evidence against it. No writer of repute writing on state and local taxation in the United States has failed to offer his bit of derogatory testimony. No commission appointed to investigate any state tax system, which has had time, means, and inclination to secure the evidence, has failed to recommend the abolition of the tax or measures tending toward fundamental modification. Where permanent administrative tax commissions have had time, capacity, and means to busy themselves with what ought to be one of their major tasks, the study and constructive criticism of the state tax system, they have without exception arrived at similar conclusions.

Yet the tax persists.[4]

Looking at the property tax today, we can apply the same criteria used in relation to the individual income tax: revenue production, economic effects, equity within and among income classes, and acceptability as a function of all these. As has been suggested, the property tax is less acceptable than the income tax, and various reasons have been used to explain this. In fact, looking at the three basic criteria, not all the criticisms are justified, but some basic ones are.

The property tax is frequently criticized, for example, because of its failure to grow as a source of revenue as fast as the need for this revenue grows. This lack of growth is attributed to lagging assessment and to a failure of the wealth base for property taxation to rise as fast as the income base for most other taxation. Netzer demonstrates that these criticisms are not well founded. He points out that during 1956–1961, the Gross National Product grew at an average annual rate of 4.3 percent, whereas assessed value of property subject to local general property taxes grew 5.5 percent a year (estimated true market value of the same property grew 7.0 percent a year, and this again indicates that discrepancies in the assessment system are at the heart of the problem of the property tax), and property tax revenue grew at the even higher rate of 8.2 percent a year.[5]

The real basis of the common feeling concerning the revenue shortcomings of the property tax then lies not in the provision of revenue by this tax nor even in the slow growth of the wealth on which it is based. It seems much more likely that the real complaint is based on the even faster growth of state and local government expenditures, 8.3 percent per year, which in turn called for the 8.2 percent increase in property tax revenue that, together with the substantially lower increase in the tax base, meant a rise in tax rates. In this case, of course, the villain is expenditure, and the property tax seems, if anything, noble in providing revenue for this expenditure.

The economic effects of the property tax are generally considered bad in the sense of distorting consumer preferences as expressed in markets, and property taxation does indeed differentially affect the application of resources to those items taxed, such as buildings, as compared ·to untaxed items. But, as pointed out in the last section, this is not peculiar to the property tax, and on this count it may stand up well even against the individual income tax. The example of the income tax and the property tax working efficiently in tandem to preserve slums is, unfortunately, not atypical.

When we come to the two kinds of equity, however, we begin to close in on the reason for the relatively low level of acceptability of the property tax. It is frequently suggested that one fault of the property tax is that it is regressive, taking a larger percentage of lower incomes than of higher and thus violating current standards of among-income-class equity. In fact, the property tax is regressive with regard to income; Netzer estimates that allowing for tax shifting from owners of rental housing to renters, the below-$2,000 income class averages a property tax rate of 3.27 percent; middle-income groups typically pay from 1.25 to 1.75 percent; and those earning more than $15,000 a year pay only 1.15 percent.[6] But the traditional explanation usually assigned for this regressivity, namely, the underassessment of higher-price houses, is denied by Netzer on the basis of several estimates.[7] Rather, he suggests that the property tax is regressive simply because lower-income receivers pay out a larger portion of their incomes on housing than do higher-income receivers. This, then, would be the same kind of regressivity associated with the sales tax (lower-income recipients consume relatively more and save less than those with higher incomes) but sales taxes are far less unpopular. The difference here is again, I think, that unlike the sales tax the property tax is assessed on property appraised by outsiders; for the low- or middle-income payer of property taxes who sees others with better property paying taxes which they are better able to pay out of their current incomes, this external assessment of an apparently unfair tax becomes close to intolerable.

This comes close to the other kind of equity, treating people in the same income classes similarly. If the property tax does not seem to treat unequal incomes unequally enough, it also seems to fail in taxing equal incomes the same. In part the apparent case is illusory. One of the major bases for the political unpopularity of the property tax is that it taxes homeowners, but not renters who have the same income, and home ownership in California, for example, shares some of the mom's apple pie mystique of conservative America. The economist suggests, however, that the property tax on owners of rental property is passed on to renters (which is why the incidence of the tax on low-income groups is high) and that this apparent inequity is not real.

In fact, allowing for market lags and imperfections, too frequently ignored by economists, the incidence of property taxes on homeowners probably is somewhat higher than on renters. But this is not the strongest part of the contention that the tax is inequitable within income classes. More important is the evidence that the assessment of the tax on different kinds and different pieces of property is spotty and inaccurate. Property values, unlike wages and most other incomes (those subject to the simple portion of the income tax), are imprecise and must be evaluated arbitrarily. From this fact comes a tide of troubles.

The National League of Cities, summarizing a conference on improving property tax assessment, not doing away with the tax (the cities must live with the property tax until someone else—the federal government or the states—provides other sources of revenue), makes the current state of assessment quite clear:

> Today the sad fact is that almost nobody realizes how bad property tax assessments are apt to be, almost nobody understands how many urban problems and housing problems are made worse by bad assessments and (worst of all) almost nobody seems to care except to hope his own property will get in on the right side of a bad assessment instead of on the wrong side. One big reason for today's assessment discrepancies is that 90 percent of today's homeowners mistakenly believe that they are getting the best of a bad deal. They are much less interested in assessment equity than in getting inequity favorable to themselves.[8]

In fact, the increasing evidence of revolt against property taxes indicates that the quotation is overoptimistic (or overpessimistic as the case may be) in the statement that "almost nobody seems to care except to hope his own property will get in on the right side," and the solutions suggested by the conference, though likely to lead to some improvement, would hardly suffice to solve a problem of the magnitude indicated by the conference itself.

Bad assessment exists (and is likely to continue) for a number of reasons:

1. Assessment is difficult, particularly in a thin property market where transactions take place infrequently. The major basis for assessment of the market value of property is price of those transactions for similar property that have taken place recently. But if transactions take place infrequently, and if property is similar but not identical, accurate assessment of the true market value of property not changing hands becomes very difficult. This is a basic reason for one of the major gripes heard about property taxes, the fact that after assessments have been level for a number of years, they suddenly jump. They jump, among other reasons, because new transactions in what is more or less the same market take place irregularly, and when they do take place, they indicate large changes in value since the last transaction.

2. There is arbitrary discrimination among classes of property for deliberate policy purposes. Assessment of business property is frequently low relative to residential property, for example, because of a policy decision to try to attract business into an area. Such a policy decision may be conceived by the assessors or other policy-makers to be in the general interest of the area, yet it is frequently implicit, necessarily arbitrary, and sometimes even misconceived as a means of attracting business.

3. There is enough evidence of nonpolicy discrimination or favoritism so that, on top of all the others, the whole thing looks like a composite of special interests. And since all this is applied to the taxpayer by someone else, there is little wonder

that the payer is frequently unhappy with the system. Assessors and other public officials set rules that look arbitrary, and then do not always follow these rules. The best of them do it in what they believe to be the public interest, but this conception of the public interest is far different from the conception of self-interest that rules in market systems.

The National League of Cities conference's solutions to all this can be summarized as greater state (as compared to local) participation in determining assessment practices, consolidation of assessment districts, and higher standards of competence and pay for assessors.[9] The last is the key, as it is the key to success for all highly administered systems. Were it possible to get the right people, get the right rules, and give the right orders, the systems would work. But at some times and places, these things have all been tried; the failure of the property tax, together with failure of practically all administered systems, provides strong inductive evidence that such ideal changes are not possible on a generalized basis.

The property tax is a highly decentralized system. It is decentralized to localities and decentralized even further because decisions are made by individual assessors within localities. And the uneven workings of this decentralized system throw substantial doubt on decentralization as a public policy ideal. What is suggested here is that the decentralization of the marketplace and of the individual income tax work relatively well because these are decentralized systems in which the motivating force is self-interest; self-interest, if not always easy to interpret, at least is generally satisfactory to the individual self. But decentralization to myriads of public policy-makers acting in what they conceive to be the public interest may work badly or not at all. At one time, a public relations man, intent on proving something or other, re-enacted the battle of Bunker Hill with the American troops represented by a team of men who had various quirks in their vision. The resultant response to the command, "Don't fire 'til you see the whites of their eyes," was a ragged and irregular rattle rather than the concentrated volley tradition assigns to the defenders of the Hill. The interpretation of laws and rules by decentralized public policy-makers frequently has a similar quality.

The Military Draft

The military draft resembles the property tax in that others determine the contribution that must be made by the young men subjected to military service. The others in this case are quasipublic officials, the members of draft boards rather than public employees, but in terms of the public-spiritedness of their objectives this seems to make little difference. And the military draft has the same kinds of drawbacks as the property tax for the same kinds of reasons. For the draft, these drawbacks are even more upsetting because the contribution called for in wartime from a draftee may be vital in a literal sense. This is one reason for the very high level of protest and agitation surrounding the draft during the Vietnam war.

The property tax is a local system with assessments locally determined; the draft is a national system decentralized to the extent that the assessments on individuals are as locally determined as the property tax. And like the property tax, the national spread of the application of the draft is very uneven indeed. It is a well-known phenomenon, for example, that deferments for students are far easier to obtain in some districts where college attendance is relatively unusual and highly respected and relatively hard to obtain in districts where colleges are located.

And like the property tax, it is difficult to determine equity under the draft. There is a maze of rules and regulations, all of which are interpreted by the local draft board, and the draft board, if not supreme, is very nearly so, subject to complex appeal procedures. The result is that in some cases, the draft board does not merely interpret the rules and regulations; it ignores them. And the situation is exacerbated by the fact that given the needs for military personnel, which are small relative to the manpower pool being drawn on, draft regulations are not used to determine exceptions to a general rule that everyone should be drafted, but rather to separate the draft-deferred sheep from the draftable goats. The sheep and goats are frequently very similar, at least physically, and the sheep are very likely to escape the draft in perpetuity.

In fact, not only is it difficult to determine equity in the draft as in the property tax, but in the draft as in the other case, there is discrimination based on policy. Some discrimination is intended; the substantially smaller likelihood of someone going to college ever being drafted is at least in part an intended result of the system. Some policy-based discrimination is unintended; it would certainly be denied that blacks are more draftable than whites, yet proportionately many more qualified blacks are drafted (14.3 percent of draftees during the late 1960s were Negroes even though only 9.2 percent of the qualified population was black).[10] This greater incidence of the draft among qualified Negroes is due to student deferments, the greater ease with which whites get into such programs as the National Guard, and so forth; the end result is that proportionately fewer whites get drafted.

And again, as in the case of the property tax, there is real personal discrimination built on top of the policy-based discrimination. There can be little doubt that many draft boards, until recently uniformly lily white, have treated Negroes differently from whites. There can be no less doubt that favoritism has been shown in various times in various places throughout the country. And again, all the discrimination becomes far more irksome because draft liability is in the final analysis imposed on one group, young men, by another, primarily old men.

The draft looked much more workable during World War II. Then it was much less of a *selective* service system; at least within the younger age groups, every male went, with exceptions based mainly on reasonably clearly defined physical and mental defects. This meant much less discrimination, much less arbitrary discretion. The discretion came in when the system needed so few men that the draft boards were forced to make real selections. And as in the case of other systems based on decentralized interpretation of the public interest rather than decentralized self-interest, the draft has moved to the margin of near unworkability, with the Vietnam war as a catalyst.

Two major alternatives have been proposed to the draft as it has been.

One, the selection by a lottery or other random mechanism, has begun. To the extent that this is successful in really substituting the workings of pure chance for the discretion of draft boards, it can be very attractive indeed. More often, however, discretionary exceptions are still made, and sheep and goats are still separated. To the extent that the lottery at least cuts down on discretion and on the discrimination that goes with discretion, it is an improvement; but the discretion that remains is still almost as onerous as that which existed before the lottery.

The other alternative in many ways looks even more attractive. It bases military recruitment not on any system of conscription, but on the market. The proposal is to raise the wages of military men until enough volunteers fill the needs of the armed services. This would be a true market system and a true decentralization based on people's determination of their own self-interest. The proposal is attractive, at least to economists, but it is still no approach to perfection. For one thing, just considering the economics of it, it is possible that there is no wage within the range of political feasibility that will induce enough men to make themselves available to be shot at. This is probably not the case; estimates made by the President's Commission on an All-Volunteer Armed Force indicate that such a force is feasible at modest additional costs.[11] Even so, these estimates were necessarily based on soft and hypothetical data, and it may just not come out that way.

The use of the free market for military recruitment brings out again one of the same basic problems caused by current uses of the free market, the problem of distributive equity. As has been suggested, the uncontrolled market does not produce an income distribution conforming to most current ideas of equity; other devices, such as income taxes, are needed. Given the income distribution produced by the free market, even as moderated somewhat by the income tax, however, the attractiveness of any given military pay rate is likely to differ very widely according to the income level and future prospects of the men of military age. To put it bluntly, those with low current and prospective incomes are likely to volunteer disproportionately at any given pay rate. If this turns out to be the case, it may imply a socially intolerable distribution of liability to the life-risking enterprise of military service, similar in kind but much harsher in degree than other distributional inequalities, and this will remain so even though the low-income volunteers are volunteers and not draftees.

In addition, substantial social and political questions are raised by the possibility of a permanent and professional large (as compared, for example, to before 1939) army, not well integrated into American society as a whole.

The argument is not an overwhelming one; the reason it is made here is to indicate again that moving toward a market system from an administered one does not solve all problems. In particular it does not solve problems of distributive equity, and indeed frequently tends to exacerbate them. In the case of the draft, my own preference is very slightly for an all-volunteer army as compared to the draft as it is now, but the considerations not taken care of by the market system are strong ones, and perhaps the cutting down of the discretionary nature of the draft through the introduction of a stricter lottery would be the best solution available. Universal youth service encompassing the military, the Peace Corps, VISTA, the Teachers Corps, and other new activities also seems attractive, if currently out of political reach.

In any case, in the draft as in the property tax and the complex portion of the individual income tax, most problems stem from the discretion of public officials trying (however sincerely) to follow the rules.

Public Assistance

In many ways the worst system within the United States is public assistance, by which the poor are kept from starvation (most of the time) through the handing out of relief monies. For the recipient of public assistance, the payments are too low to prevent much more than starvation, and the means by which they are laid out by welfare officials are frequently demeaning to the point of brutality. For the payer of the taxes that support welfare, it is too expensive, and what is worse, the system is spiraling out of control with nobody having a sure idea of how to cut back even on the rate of increase in the number of public assistance recipients.

The public assistance system, like the property tax, is administered by local public officials making discretionary decisions; like the draft these decisions are made by interpreting or ignoring a set of national rules. Public assistance is perhaps the most decentralized of all these systems since the ultimate discretion (subject as always to inadequate appeal) is in the hands of an individual welfare worker.

Since the argument here is that the faults of public assistance are due in substantial measure to this inadequate administration, it may be best first to dispose in part of one attractive piece of evidence ostensibly in favor of my argument. It is possible to compare public assistance to the other portion of the basic income maintenance system of the United States, Social Security. The Social Security pension system is popular, smooth, and efficient; it is also virtually automatic in its workings, like the income tax, and is administered with relatively little discretion by public officials. It would be easy to contrast the unhappy public assistance system with the happy Social Security system and to suggest that the difference can be credited to the lack of discretionary administration in the latter. These administrative differences, however, cannot be separated from another major difference, that of the clientele of the two systems. Social Security is an inclusive system, and its recipients are primarily white, middle class, and voters who come from the same families as the majority of Americans. Public assistance, particularly the most controversial portion, Aid to Families with Dependent Children, is for the exceptions, and its recipients are disproportionately black, lower class, and with standards of morality frequently questioned by the majority. In other words, Social Security is "Us," public assistance "Them," and it is impossible to separate out this difference as a cause of the differential workability of the system from the administrative difference. The fact that those portions of public assistance that go to people more like Us—Old Age Assistance and Aid to the Blind, for example—seem to work better than Aid to Families with Dependent Children, which goes largely to minority-group poor, indicates that administrative factors do not stand alone in causing the difficulties of public assistance. The relatively smooth working of the veterans' pension system, which is discretionary, is a similar indication.

In any case, however, the specific drawbacks caused by discretionary administration of the public assistance system can be singled out. Indeed, the public assistance system is the first one discussed here that may be said to be a result of bad planning as well as bad administration. Public assistance was planned initially to work in a certain way, and the planners had reasonable expectations which have remained signally unfulfilled. Public assistance, as begun during the 1930s, was expected to be a residual program for the unfortunate who were down on their luck, providing them with temporary relief, with aid to get back on their feet, and with the comfort and guidance of welfare workers. During 1962, when it had become quite clear that the system was not working this way (it was rather a self-perpetuating generation-to-generation system for too many people, tending to keep people on relief rather than getting them off), the law was amended to provide even more aid and comfort from welfare workers. It worked worse that way.

The system works badly for three general kinds of reasons:

1. Unlike any of the systems discussed so far, public assistance is based in large measure on concepts that, according to at least some frequently accepted current value systems, could be called just plain ill will. That is, it is based in some measure on a desire to separate those needing public support from those who can support themselves and to punish the former. This was certainly not the intention of the New Dealers who designed it, but it has been the more explicit intention of some of those who administered the system at one level or another and of those who have occasionally amended it. It is the root cause of

some of the worst administrative features of the system, such as the man-in-the-house investigation, which started out as an effort to enforce zealously the rules that allowed payments only for families with female heads not supported by a man, and deteriorated in many cases to an investigation of the morals of the recipient.

2. The system works badly because the planners ignored the power of self-interest among the poor and worked out a set of rules that provided strong incentives for the perpetuation of the welfare status. Until recently, the rules were such that any earnings brought in by a person on welfare would take away dollar for dollar from relief payments, thus providing no monetary incentive to work and get off the system. Until recently, the strength of enforcement of the man-in-the-house rule was such that the incentive was for the family to break up and the legitimate father to leave because as long as he was in the house, the family would starve without relief payments. Presumably, the planners who thought of the system just did not happen to think about these perverse incentives. And this is a sad commentary indeed on the state of public planning.

3. The most important factor concerning the mechanics through which other factors work is the fact that the public assistance system is locally administered. The federal standards for welfare are not all bad (even in spite of the occasional lapses such as the incentives not to work and to break up families), but these broad standards are interpreted by state officials (decentralized and acting in the public interest rather than self-interest) and typically administered by county welfare departments. Finally, they are applied by individual welfare workers, only some of whom are reasonably well trained. The result of this is that many states are low in their payments, particularly in the South; many counties are harsh in application of the rules, and not only in the South. Contra Costa County in California, for example, was applying standards of eligibility not only harshly, but as demonstrated in court, illegitimately, for quite some time. And, finally, the welfare workers with whom the recipients have their prime contact are sometimes harsh and, when not harsh, all too frequently paternalistic, treating

recipients as children who need their thinking done for them, an attitude not conducive to self-reliance.

The result of this system of decentralized public interest administration is that even though some of the worst aspects, like the antiwork and antifamily incentives, may change, by rule or by law, any new system operated through the same administrative apparatus is likely to have far too much resemblance to the old system, as welfare workers interpret regulations within rules within laws. The honest civil servant, who is clearly in the vast majority, follows the rules as best he knows how, but following the system's hierarchy of rules within laws, he frequently ends up by reversing the real intent of the system by 180 degrees.[12]

President Nixon's Family Assistance Plan gives some promise of changing all this in the right direction; it is a substitute for the welfare system that redoes many of the basic rules and regulations. Much less remarked on than the new substantive rules, but perhaps even more important, however, is the fact that Family Assistance changes the method of administration from the federal-state-local structure described here to a semiautomatic mode similar to Social Security and is enforced by sampling, as is the federal income tax. The new system carries with it incentives to the states to allow the federal government to take on the entire administration of this and other welfare programs. If this change in administration is bought by the states it will be a more important favorable change than all the rest.

Two Other Federal-State-Local Systems: Education and Manpower

Public assistance is so burdened with guilt, racial feeling, and moral imperatives that it may not be considered a good example of the difficulties involved in administering a federal-state-local system. In fact, it probably is; its other burdens may exaggerate the administrative drawbacks, but this only enables us to see these drawbacks better. For confirmation, however, it is useful to look at two other federal-state-local systems: federal aid to education and the federal-state-local manpower system.

Federal aid to education was begun on a comprehensive basis during 1965 when President Johnson proposed and Congress passed the first major bill of this type. In considering the administrative drawbacks discussed here, then, it is important to remember that the entire concept of federal aid to education was hung up for nearly twenty years over such issues as church versus state and local control of education. If any bill were to be passed at all, it probably had to be this bill, with all its faults. Nonetheless, the severe limitations on decentralized local control of such a program are well illustrated by the workings of federal aid to education.

Title I of the Elementary and Secondary Education Act, with which this discussion is concerned, extends federal aid to school districts having concentrations of low-income disadvantaged students. Though the aid is extended to the districts, it is defined in terms of aid to the students; this was the device that broke through the church versus state and other issues. Funds are allocated to states and to districts through a formula stressing the number of recipients of Aid to Families with Dependent Children. The funds flow through the state to the districts, and the state must approve or disapprove the specific projects proposed by the districts for the use of the federal monies.

The way this has worked out must be understood in the context of the historically high degree of local jealousy over the prerogatives of local school districts. Local school superintendents and principals have always fought hard against interference with their rights to run their own schools; because of their numerical and organizational power, they have generally been quite successful in these battles. The local control ethos conditioned the way the federal aid bill was written, and it conditions the way it has been applied. In principle, the federal Department of Health, Education and Welfare, which administers the program, has the right to enforce the rules it has set and to evaluate the programs for which the monies are spent. But in practice, the federal government has not even been completely successful in enforcing the basic rule of the program, namely, that the monies should be spent on improving the education of disadvantaged children. It also has had very little success in enforcing any other standards and has been almost completely unable to evaluate the resulting educational projects.

One reason for the department's impotence is that the informal professional structure of educational bureaucrats, extending from the federal Office of Education down through the local school administrative hierarchies, is stronger than the formal rules. For reasons ranging from professional doctrine through political peace-keeping, the professionals at any level are reluctant to rock the boat, yet Title I, to effect change, must do considerable rocking. For similar reasons, then, there is little supervision of the local programs by most state educational authorities, and at the local level there is little capability or desire to think through carefully what programs might be most helpful in achieving the compensatory education objectives of the federal aid. (To be fair to the current set of local authorities, however, there is virtually no knowledge about what works in compensatory education for disadvantaged children.[13] In large measure, this is because previous generations of local authorities, preserving their prerogatives, resisted systematic comparative evaluation, but at any rate, it cannot be blamed directly on current authorities.)

In any case, the result of the diffusion of operating and evaluative authority under this loose application of the federal-state-local system has resulted in the fact that after four years, no demonstration has been made that the federal expenditure of $5–10 billion has had any results whatever in improving the education of the students whom it was to aid. If the goal of the Title I program was general fiscal aid and relief for school districts, typically in difficult financial straits, this goal has been reached in a small degree, because $1 billion a year of Title I funds is only a small increment on $40 billion or so of state and local spending on education. But in any case, no measurable changes in the achievements of needy students are observable. And, as a general statement, the cause of this failure has been an extreme degree of federal-state-local decentralization with rules not likely to be followed, with no incentives to school authorities to follow the rules, and with no criteria to examine whether either the rules have been followed or the results have been those intended.

Unlike the federal-state-local education system, the federal-state-local manpower and training system has been built slowly over time. The federal-state-local employment service was created on a permanent basis during the New Deal period. It was to be run by the states and financed by the federal government out of the small fraction of state-collected unemployment insurance taxes that were turned over to the federal government. The initial purpose of the employment service was primarily to administer the new unemployment insurance system and the new job-finding system for those receiving employment compensation.

Over the years, the federal-state employment services have broadened to become more general employment agencies. And like most employment agencies, the reward system is based on successful placements, so the services have become oriented toward satisfying the employers by supplying employees of the type desired by employers. An employment agency is dependent on employer good will for its business; if it supplies employees whom the employer thinks are unqualified, it is in trouble. Many employers have believed that black or other minority group employees, or those with other kinds of disadvantages, have been automatically underqualified, and in many cases the state unemployment services have been willing to go along with this.

During 1962, the Manpower Development and Training Act created the Manpower Administration within the U.S. Department of Labor. The Manpower Administration was a small centralized bureaucracy imposed on top of a Holy Roman Empire which included not only the fifty autonomous state employment services, but also numerous other Labor Department bureaus, each with its own constituency and political power. The primary functions of the Manpower Administration were the channeling of federal manpower funds (which might have given it considerable leverage were it not for the political power of the fund receivers at the state and the bureau level) and planning. In regard to the federal-state employment services, the

Manpower Administration initially adapted itself in large measure by becoming the creature of the state agencies.

It was this double system that during 1964, as the attention of the country focused on the War on Poverty, was supposed to turn its attention to the manpower needs of the poor and of the minority groups. And this was really the first time the attention of the employment service had been so focused. As suggested above, previous to 1964, the orientation had been on supplying good workers to employers, and, for a brief time between 1962 and 1964, on retraining of workers whose skills had become obsolete (for example, coal miners, packing-house workers), a quite different matter from the basic training programs needed by the poor. And what was needed for the War on Poverty was a shift to a recognition of the requirements of the client groups in poverty and a flexible set of programs applicable to a wide variety of needs in a variety of economic settings.

What came out was close to the reverse. Because the new Manpower Administration superstructure was in itself centralized, its planning mechanism tended to produce program models with the expectation that they would work if reproduced in detail throughout the country. Because the Manpower Administration wanted to gain real control over its collection of principalities, it tried to use antipoverty funds as an instrument (which, as noted, worked only imperfectly, because of the political power of the local princes). And, oddly enough, because the Manpower Administrators were sincere in their antipoverty commitment, they used adherence to the set programs of their planners as the touchstone for obtaining federal funds.

As a result, throughout the early years of the War on Poverty, from 1964 through 1967, the Manpower Administration in Washington supplied a set of canned programs based on a single model in Chicago, which had been supposed to be successful but had not really been tested, and told the local operators that only these programs would be funded. And the state employment services in most states found it difficult to move toward the poverty orientation needed to obtain jobs for the recipients of the training programs under the new dispensation; even though the focus had changed in Washington, the bureaucratic incentive structure of the local state employment services was still tied to employer approbation, and employers were not ready to wholeheartedly take on the poor. Nor, given the quality of the training programs the poor were coming out of, should they have been. The result of all this, then, was a set of rigid and ineffectual training programs without much increase in the chance of obtaining a job at the end of the program for those of the poverty groups who had been through the programs. Not surprisingly, it all worked very poorly.

Again, this was a case of decentralization within rules. Indeed, in this case, it was more than rules, it was precise directives as to what a program should look like. Again, the rules were more or less followed, but with no incentive to get the results intended for the rules. Again, decentralization through a system of public officials making decisions in what they perceived to be the public good worked very poorly indeed.

Systems Involving Comprehensive Planning

The first three systems discussed in this chapter, the business-market economy, the anti–business-cycle system, and the federal individual income tax, are nonadministered systems in the sense that they work primarily through the decentralized decision-making of individuals acting in their own self-interest. They are also unplanned except in the broadest way. The second set contains administered systems—the property tax, the draft, the public assistance system, and the federal-state-local educational and manpower systems—each run through sets of rules interpreted by public authorities acting not in their self-interest but in what they believe to be the public interest. The systems in the second category, however, though some, such as education and manpower, may involve planning for future actions on more than a day-to-day basis, do not call for anything approaching comprehensive planning. Their objectives and functions are limited, covering only narrow ranges of activities. The third category, then, picks up systems that are intended to carry out comprehensive planning. The cases here are the National Recovery Administration of the early New Deal, which was intended as an attempt to plan the whole economy (though not even the attempt was ever really made), the War Production Board of the 1940s, and the Urban Renewal Program of the 1950s and early 1960s, which was in large measure an attempt to improve urban communities through comprehensive planning.

The National Recovery Administration (*NRA*)

The 1920s were the heyday of the free operations of the business-market system. The system worked, providing economic progress for most Americans. Because it worked and seemed to work smoothly, it was popular and seldom questioned. During 1924, Calvin Coolidge ("The Business of America Is Business") received a majority of 54 percent of the popular vote over two opponents in the Presidential election. The "Great Engineer," Herbert Hoover, received 59 percent during 1928.

Of the two questions raised at the beginning of this chapter concerning the failures of the business-market system, one did not seem relevant during the 1920s: the business cycle. Certainly the cycle was in operation, but through 1929 its turns were acceptable. During 1929, the national unemployment rate was 3.2 percent, very low by current standards. Unemployment was not thought of as a chronic problem of the economy, but as a necessary corrective. And what protests there were about the workings of the economy during the 1920s were based on the other drawback typical of such economies, the failure to provide distributive equity. Those who felt that the system produced an income distribution so unequal as to be inequitable were in a minority, however. The value system of the 1920s differed from today's, and the majority seemed to feel that rewarding producers according to their productive contribution was the only rule needed; greater income equality had little or nothing to do with it.

In any case, the economic system worked and worked smoothly and that made it easy to defend. During 1929, it stopped working and in doing so brought both the cycle and the equity problems to crisis. During 1933, the inauguration of Franklin Roosevelt as President began the New Deal efforts at trying to solve the problems brought about by a freely working private market economy. The first thrust of the New Deal measures was a set of emergency economic and relief measures designed primarily just to hold things together past the crises of the next few days, weeks, or months. The last set of New Deal measures, concentrated primarily in Roosevelt's second term, 1937 through 1941, attacked the failures of the economic system in ways that are still reflected today. The business cycle itself was attacked by an increasingly self-conscious (but too small to be effective) application of compensatory policy of the type discussed above. The inequities produced by the economy were attacked by the use of the income tax system discussed above, as well as the use of collective bargaining, which will be discussed later.

In between the first emergency measures and the ultimate workings out of the New Deal, however, came the first general noncrisis attempt to solve the economic problems of the Depression. This was intended as a design for national planning. The Depression was most certainly due to the uncontrolled and unplanned workings of the business-market economy. Therefore, the appealing syllogism went, it could be cured and future depressions prevented by controlling and planning this economy. Indeed, if planning is defined broadly enough, the syllogism has since turned out to be true; the planning of the broad workings of compensatory fiscal and monitory policy has enabled us to avoid extreme depression as well as extreme inflation.

But this is not what the planning advocates of the early 1930s meant. In fact, they did not really know what they did mean aside from feeling that planning was good. The major legislative expression of the drive to plan was the National Industrial Recovery Act passed by Congress in June 1933, toward the end of Roosevelt's famous one hundred days. The act had two elements. Title II set up a system of public works to employ the unemployed, an early attempt at what today would be considered standard countercyclical policy. To the chagrin of Gen. Hugh Johnson, who administered the rest of the act and thought he was to administer this too, Title II was cut out from under him by Roosevelt and given to Harold Ickes, the Secretary of the Interior. At this point, Title II drops out of the relevant part of the story.

Title I of the act set up a system whereby cartel-like industry and business associations were to design codes of fair competition, using these codes to create standards for doing business in a way that would avoid what was thought to be destructive competition, which many believed to be at the root of the depression. The code for each industry had to be approved or disapproved by a new federal agency set up by President Roosevelt, the National Recovery Administration (NRA), headed by Gen. Johnson. The NRA could use several weapons for enforcement. For one thing, the cooperative creation of such codes by trade associations clearly violated the antitrust laws, and only the NRA had the right to suspend these laws when it accepted a code. In addition, the government had further enforcing power through a procedure by which it could license firms to do business; this was inherently great power indeed, but it was never used. Finally, perhaps the major sanction was the use of public opinion to enforce the codes. The NRA created the famous Blue Eagle seal, which was granted to firms that promised to abide by the agreed-on codes for their industry. It was hoped that the public would refuse to buy from a company from which the Blue Eagle had been withheld.

The codes, as they worked out, contained two types of regulations. One of these set minimum standards for working conditions, production, and, particularly important, collective bargaining. The other type moved toward the direct fixing of prices and outputs. The two parts of the code worked quite differently. The minimum standards, which primarily concerned social aspects of production, such as child labor and collective bargaining, were fought hard by many industries. But the prohibition of child labor and encouragement of collective bargaining were insisted on by the NRA and were grudgingly accepted by most companies. For child labor, this was the beginning of the end in the United States; for collective bargaining, it was the beginning of the beginning which was later structured through the passage of the National Labor Relations Act after the National Industrial Recovery Act had been declared unconstitutional. These minimum standards, in fact, were little different from the kinds of constraints that had long existed on the forms that could be taken by self-interest in the market economy. It has never been legal, for example, to steal patents or private copyrights, but this has not been considered an interference with the free market. The minimum standards of the National Industrial Recovery Act were little different from these older constraints.

The story of the attempt to stabilize the economy by letting industrial trade associations set prices and production quotas is quite different. Indeed, it is different from the kind of centralization usually implied by the phrase "government planning." Planning by industrial groups had long been carried on by European cartels and in the U.S. sub rosa through trust and monopoly arrangements, and though the designers of NRA intended the government role to prevent European-style cartelization, this was the kind of planned production that American business wanted. The price setting it implied was setting at a high level, and the production setting was a level low enough to sell the entire product at the high price. Business, then, wanted to set high prices. The government, on the other hand, did not really know what it wanted. What it seemed to come to was that the government wanted high prices to producers in order to prevent wage cutting, business failure, and further retreat into depression. But the government also wanted low prices to consumers in order to promote sales, production, and employment. High prices to business and low prices to consumers were not compatible, and in addition, the government, or at least many people within the government, also wanted to avoid government price fixing as such and were dubious about monopolistic price fixing. The result of all this made many in the government unhappy because initially business seemed to be getting its way unhampered. According to Arthur Schlesinger, Jr.:

What had begun as an effort to check the downward spiral seemed now to turn in the hands of code authorities into a monstrous new apparatus by which business could keep production down and prices up. In the end, it was thought, the business community, in its pursuit of profits and security for each separate industry, might well create a situation where recovery for all would be impossible.[14]

This dilemma was never really resolved. What the recovery codes turned out to be were partial price fixing by business, partially enforced. Toward the end of NRA (it was declared unconstitutional by the Supreme Court in 1936), the price-fixing codes were pretty nearly dead letters. This kind of provision had proven unworkable, though NRA went out of business for other reasons.

The concern here, in any case, is not with constitutional history, but with administrative devices; not why NRA was unconstitutional, but why this decentralized variety of planning and price-fixing aspects did not work. As Schlesinger put it: "By holding prices at artificial levels, industry, in its pursuit of short-run profits, prevented the 'increasing volume of goods and services' which alone could end unemployment." [15] And the reason for this, as stated by George Leighton of *Harper's* Magazine and quoted by Schlesinger was that: "Any supposition that business intends to 'govern itself' in the spirit of the New Deal, is preposterous. The profit motive is still solidly in the saddle." [16] This was the basic problem. The profit motive was still in the saddle because business was still business. The planning enthusiasts of the early New Deal thought of price in several ways. They thought of price as a cyclical control, albeit without having solved the high-price-to-business low-price-to-consumers dilemma. It was later pointed out by John Maynard Keynes that the dilemma created by the fact that prices and wages are income to some people and costs to others is an insoluble one that makes price variation ineffective as countercyclical policy, but this *was* later.

In addition to price as a cyclical control, the early planners thought of price as a device in equity to get everybody his fair share. This concept still exists today in the farm parity system, which dates from the same period. Parity is the ratio of prices paid to farmers to prices paid by farmers. Since most parity payments now go to rich farmers, it is quite clear that parity is not much of a creator of equity.

In any case, in using price to try to cure the business cycle and inequity flaws of the market system, the planners of the 1930s made it difficult for price to perform its real function in a market system, as the rationer and allocator of goods and services. And without price, there was no device for allocation. Neither industry nor the government could set prices and production in a way that allowed any hope that the parts would fit together and the economy work. The equations to be solved were simply too complex, and nobody tried. Nor could industry or government do away with the self-interest that caused some businessmen to sell below the artificially high prices. During the NRA period, the price cutters were called chiselers, just as during World War II, those who got around rationing by selling goods at prices above the fixed ones were called black marketers. Neither of these epithets is pleasant, but the use of unpleasant epithets failed to do away with the self-interest that made the NRA price- and production-fixing system unworkable. No more than government officials acting in what they believed to be the public good could trade associations acting in what they believed to be the collective good of their industry do away with the power of the individual self-interest of the businessmen directly concerned. The centralized planning failed by failing to take account of the self-interest incentives that made the market system run.

World War II Planning and Controls

The planning intended by the designers of NRA turned out not to be centralized planning, and indeed in the final analysis, not to be planning at all. The handling of the American economy and American industry during World War II provides a much stronger example of actual centralized planning of a highly administered system, planning that in large measure substituted for the free market economy. Under the wartime goad, the planned system worked moderately well, but certainly not well enough that anybody would propose the reinstitution of such a system except under the extreme pressures of wartime.

Perhaps the first question about World War II planning and controls should be why it was done at all. If the free market and price system work so well, why were they not used to bring to wartime production the efficiency they are supposed to bring in peacetime? In principle, after all, it would be possible to give purchasers of military goods enough spending power to bid on the market for the production they need and to prevent inflation by cutting down on other spending power (primarily that of consumers) by heavy taxation or by forced saving through such devices as compulsory bond purchases. Under such a free market war system, planners would merely have to do the top-level job of laying out a set of military needs and designating a balance between military and civilian production; the price system would then follow up, carrying out through its ordinary workings the task of allocating raw materials, components, labor, and equipment to produce the final set of military and consumer goods. This is just about what the price system does in peacetime for the consumption-dominated economy.

In fact, such a use of the price-market system, though it certainly has its advantages as compared to wartime controls, is impossible for several reasons. One of these has been mentioned above in the discussion of business cycle control. This is the difficulty of reconciling price-as-allocator with equity in a time of war shortages, the dilemma of unequal income distribution leading to extreme hardship, on the one hand, and income equalization leading to erosion of the incentives needed for allocation, on the other. And a second reason for avoiding the price system for allocation during the war is simply the slow response that such a system would provide. In principle, the system might work, but it would work through the change in productive patterns of businessmen responding to price incentives and the change of jobs and location by workers responding to wage incentives, and these inevitably would be too slow for wartime.[17]

So the question is not whether a peacetime free market system is appropriate for wartime; clearly it is not. Rather, the important question for purposes of this study is that of the lessons the World War II system provides for peacetime.

The wartime control system was run by a number of agencies: the Office of Price Administration managed price control and rationing; the War Labor Board took care of wage control and related labor matters; other minor boards and agencies covered lesser aspects of the civilian side of the war effort. The central task, however, was that of the War Production Board (WPB), whose twofold job was to increase production and to allocate production, both between military and civilian uses (and others as lend lease), and, guided by military priorities, among military uses. The war production effort began during 1940 (under WPB's predecessor agency, the Office of Production Management) with the preparation for America's role as "Arsenal of Democracy"; it ended during 1945–1946 with postwar reconversion. And perhaps the most interesting point to note is that within this six-year period the planning and control mechanism did not really reach satisfactory operating form until mid-1943, three years after it began.

By mid-1943, the planning and control operation had to be satisfactory or the war production effort might well have collapsed. Through 1940–1941, the production problem was for the most part not one of having to make real allocation decisions, tough choices of the sort where making more of one product meant making less of another. For most strategic materials, there was enough around or producible for most high-priority needs. The problem was one of time priorities (doing first things first) together with the related problem of scheduling so that the parts came together in a timely fashion to make the whole. These were basically coordination problems. And after 1943, supplies of many key materials, which had been short, went up and stringency problems eased off somewhat. But late 1942 and 1943 were crucial. Demands of great importance to the war effort had increased to the point where they substantially exceeded supplies in some cases; the later increase of supply capabilities had not yet come to pass. Choices had to be made, and planning and control mechanisms were necessary to make these choices.

This timing was reflected within the War Production Board in a controversy over concepts of allocation. The crucial difference was between horizontal and vertical allocation of materials. Horizontal allocation was oriented around raw materials and intermediate components, and horizontal allocators asked the question: "Given a supply capability for these goods, which orders should be filled first with the highest priority?" The assumption for the most part was that all orders or at least all crucial orders could ultimately be filled, and the basic issue was thus one of scheduling. But, as high-priority demands on limited supplies increased through 1942, the necessity became acute for finding a way to allocate between alternative high-priority uses. What was critical here was the relative importance of end uses: the priorities between civilian and military; the priorities among tanks, airplanes and destroyers. And this new stress led in turn to far more stress on vertical allocation, by which the military importance of the end use determined the priority of the final product, and this priority was in turn sent down the system to component and raw material suppliers.

It is for this kind of problem that the price system works best, but as has been noted the use of the price system for this job in wartime is impossible. In 1942, there was some discussion of using a market-like system with warrants as a kind of currency to be provided prime suppliers by the military and to be passed down by the prime suppliers to their suppliers, and so forth. However, this was finally dismissed after a certain amount of experimentation. A near-market system without price to equalize supply and demand (and nobody suggested actual bidding with warrants) turned out to require almost infinite amounts of paper.

What finally was arrived at in 1942–1943, then, was the basically vertical Controlled Materials Plan (CMP). CMP retained the market-like characteristic of transmitting demands down from end-product priorities to component and material supplies, and planning for production of these lower-level supplies on the basis of actual demands rather than trying to solve a set of simultaneous planning equations for all levels at once. In addition, CMP was used only for three crucial materials: steel, aluminum and copper. Though primarily vertical in concept, the plan necessarily had to work within the supplies available of each of the three commodities, and thus required continuous horizontal juggling to make things come out right. In a true price system the juggling would have been unnecessary because if demands exceeded supplies price would have come up and the less urgent demands would have dropped by the wayside. This was, of course, impossible in the wartime control system.

So CMP was very much a system of planned and controlled production. It was a substitute for the free market of the peacetime economy, but perhaps the most important point to be made concerning comprehensive planning was that such planning only began to work adequately during 1942–1943 when the move from the previously dominant horizontal schemes of allocation to the more vertical CMP meant the utilization of market-like devices for purposes of translation of higher demands to lower. Self-interest was not involved (the patriotic incentives of wartime substituted to a great degree), but planning could not abandon the market completely.

And finally, it must be noted that even this degree of comprehensive planning worked only because it was confined to the three basic commodities; it is generally agreed by students of the effort that expansion would have swamped it.[18]

But the most important fact is that the system, though it did use some market devices, was basically a substitute for the free market system and worked moderately well in wartime. As put by Novick, Anshen, and Truppner:

It has been appraised in retrospect as an effective administrative instrument, and it earned that judgment. It did not, however, fulfill all the anticipations of its begetters. At least some of the supporters of the plan had expected to control all important war production through management of the distribution of a small group of basic materials.[19]

It did work, then, to fulfill most of the reasonable expectations of its planners. Whether it worked well as measured against some abstract model is very difficult to say. Indeed, Novick et al. suggest that this is impossible to measure:

> A policy is framed and executed. Was it good or bad? Were the results worthwhile? Was the technique of implementation efficient? How are these questions to be answered in objective terms? Private business has its dollar accounting, yielding quantitative, additive, and comparable measures of profit and loss. But most applications of government policy do not make a specific record of achievement in common units of measure. There is no evidence of the appropriateness of a particular administrative procedure which carries the conviction of positive achievement in dollars and cents. No standard has been developed as an alternative to dollar profits. There is no yardstick of demonstrable proof other than logic and the voice of the individual proponent of a particular practice in a specific situation.[20]

But the lesson for the nonwartime operation of control systems is pretty clearly that this sort of operation is workable only in wartime. This is true for two major reasons: (1) the wartime spirit, which almost alone in modern times seems capable of encouraging the cooperative sacrifice of self-interest motivation that induces people to put national goals over their individual goals; (2) the wartime ethos that defines waste differently than it is defined either for peacetime consumer production or for peacetime government programs. The universal feeling during World War II was that the goods had to be produced and though waste, corruption, and the like were followed and exposed by such instrumentalities as Senator Harry Truman's investigating committee, there was no disposition to put aside the goal of winning the war because of waste. A peacetime government effort with that degree of waste might well have been given up as impossible.

Urban Renewal

The Urban Renewal Program provides an excellent example of the failure of both national and urban planners to really understand or utilize process in their plans. The Housing Act of 1949, a broad-based bill sponsored not only by liberal legislators but also by Sen. Robert Taft, set up an Urban Redevelopment Program designed to change the outer and inner aspects of cities through a process based on planned development. The basic act was amended in 1954 (when the name was changed to Urban Renewal) and again in 1956 to put in more planning, among other things.

The Urban Renewal Act had two basic kinds of objectives: to renew the innards of central cities, which even by 1949 could be seen to be dying and needed injections of new buildings, new business, and new life; and to renew housing, to assist in the national goal of clearing out slums and providing decent housing for all Americans. A direct attack on poverty was not one of the objectives of the law, though a reasonable interpretation of the provisions for clearing out slums and rehousing slum dwellers would relate them closely to such an attack on poverty.

And it should be made clear that though there was no explicit antipoverty objective in the program, housing, particularly rehousing of slum dwellers, was an explicit objective. Because the Urban Renewal Program has signally failed in its housing objectives, some program advocates occasionally question whether housing was ever really a primary goal. In fact, in the early congressional debates in the beginning of the program, there was some ambiguity over this issue. But it is quite clear that whatever the intentions of the orators and legislators, they were not to clear out slums and ignore slum dwellers; such legislation never would have passed. As put by former Urban Renewal Commissioner William Slayton, a strong defender of the program,

In enacting Title I, the Congress recognized that slum clearance and redevelopment must involve more than assembling blighted parcels, demolishing the structures, and disposing of the land. It rightly insisted that it is a public responsibility to rehouse displaced families in decent, safe, and sanitary dwellings within their financial means. It also recognized that the eligible cost of a redevelopment project should include the costs of site improvements and supporting facilities provided by the locality—the public improvements necessary to create a stable neighborhood and support private re-construction. Finally, it required the locality to prepare a plan for the area that would guide its redevelopment and be consistent with the general plan for the community as a whole.[21]

And it is really quite clear (though not admitted in so many words by Slayton) that the Urban Renewal Program has simply failed on these counts of rehousing, creation of stable neighbor-hoods, and effective planning. The triumphs of urban renewal have been triumphs in substituting beautiful downtown office buildings and luxurious apartment houses for dirty old slums, for example, in downtown Philadelphia and Pittsburgh and in the west end of Boston. But these have been projects that far from doing anything for the previous occupants of these areas, have by and large tossed them out in favor of new and better-off occupants.

Probably the strongest and best-known opponent of the Urban Renewal Program is Martin Anderson, a professor at Columbia University at the time he made the criticisms, who has since served a term on President Nixon's White House staff. Anderson sums up the results of urban renewal as fol-lows:

> More homes were destroyed than were built. Those destroyed were predominantly low-rent homes. Those built were predomi-nantly high-rent homes. Housing conditions were made worse for those whose housing conditions were least good. Housing condi-tions were improved for those whose housing conditions were best.[22]

His description is accurate, but his reasoning explaining these dismal results is less cogent. Anderson says that:

> Since 1949, two different methods have been used to grapple with the "problems" of housing and cities. One of these is basically the system of free enterprise, guided by the complex interplay of the marketplace. The other force is the federal urban renewal pro-gram, guided by overall plans prepared by city planning experts and backed up with the taxpayers' money and the police power of the government.
> The facts tell us that private enterprise has made enormous

gains, while the federal program has not. Contrast, for example, the fantastic increase of 18 million homes in areas outside urban renewal projects with the net decrease of homes within urban renewal projects. Consider also the decrease in low-rent housing and the increase in high-rent housing in the urban renewal areas; urban renewal actually subsidizes high-income groups and hurts low-income groups. Add to this the destruction of businesses and the forcible displacement of people from their homes. The program endangers the right of private property—commercial and residential—in its equating of public interest with public use.[23]

But in fact, the Urban Renewal Program is not a substitute for the market, nor is it a federal monolith. Criticizing Anderson, Robert P. Groberg says:

> Another myth incorporated into *The Federal Bulldozer* is that there is a separate, monolithic "federal urban renewal program" run from Washington by decree. The author completely misunderstands that urban renewal is a local program. He makes it appear that the power to plan, acquire, and prepare project sites for redevelopment or rehabilitation is vested in the Federal Government and based on an opinion of the United States Supreme Court. He does not recognize that the Federal Government cannot initiate any project. He does not mention that there can be no urban renewal project anywhere unless:
> a state legislature has first adopted an enabling law to give cities the government power for urban renewal, and some forty-eight states have;
> an elected city council has first organized an operating local renewal agency, and some 800 cities have;
> the same city council has first approved the project; and some 1,600 projects have been so approved;
> the local government has first authorized local public expenditures to supplement federal funds, and more than one billion dollars in local public funds have been so approved to back the program;
> local citizens are participating in the urban renewal process, as required by law, and citizens everywhere are so doing.[24]

And Anderson is wrong, the program is a market program; Groberg is right, it is decentralized. In fact, this is at the base of the problems with urban renewal; it uses the instrumentalities and shibboleths of decentralization and private enterprise and uses them badly. Because the instrumentalities are powerful ones, their misdirection leads to powerful mistakes of the kind described by Anderson.

The Urban Renewal Program operates at three levels: the federal level, which sets the general rules and gives out the money; the local official level, which does the planning and sets up the programs; and the local private level, which carries out the programs, does the land-clearing, and builds and owns the structures that result. As pointed out by Groberg, the federal level is ineffectual. As pointed out by neither Anderson nor Groberg, however, the local official level is effective, and it is this effectiveness as much as anything else that perverts the purposes of the program. The key to local planning under urban renewal is that in order for such planning to be realistic, it must operate politically within the forces structuring city politics. And city politics in most cities is still structured very heavily by private and special interests with little concern for such matters as rehousing slum dwellers. If local planners wanted the federal Urban Renewal funds in order to revive their downtown areas, it was quite clear that they too would have to downgrade the interests of those who live in the slums to be cleared out. Too much concern here with the noble intentions of the law would likely have ended up with windmill tilting instead of programs.

So what it comes down to is that the set of forces operating through the self-interest of the construction industry and other private interests saw a possibility for profit through the Urban Renewal bill. The law did change the incentive structure so that private industry was brought into slum clearance and into the building of offices and luxury apartments. It did not change the incentive structure so that private industry was brought into rehousing slum dwellers. As put by William Grigsby,

The principal objection from which nearly all the specific criticisms flow is that the present program gives inadequate consideration to the realities of the residential real estate market, particularly as they apply to the housing needs of the low-income population. As a consequence, it has produced rather little overall improvement in living conditions per dollar of public investment. The market offers certain measures of social and economic usefulness. Its inability to reflect accurately at all times the entire array of values held by society has resulted in the rejection of many important market criteria in the planning and effectuation of urban renewal programs. Unfortunately, other measureable criteria have not been substituted for those displaced. Despite the postures assumed by planning and redevelopment agencies, however, market forces continue to operate and only too frequently produce unanticipated and undesirable consequences.[25]

And these are the lessons of the Urban Renewal Program:

1. That market forces are indeed powerful.
2. That adjustment of incentives can change the thrust of market forces and thus effect different results than would have occurred from the absolute free workings of the private market.
3. That it is very difficult to do everything through the private market and private incentives. In particular, the market is a poor place to find distributive equity.
4. That planners who plan to use the private market had better think through what they are doing more carefully than in the case of Urban Renewal. The dependence on such slogans as decentralization, federalism, and private markets is hardly preferable to the dependence on the slogans of planners who lay out the results but do not bother about laying out the route from here to there.

Bargaining Systems

Collective Bargaining under the National Labor Relations Act (NLRA)

Possibly the best known portion of the National Industrial Recovery Act of 1933 (NIRA), and certainly the one with the longest lasting effect, was Section 7A, which guaranteed the right of labor to organize and bargain collectively with employers. As the NRA began to fade, anxiety to preserve Section 7A and to strengthen it by taking advantage of the experience of the first years grew. The NIRA had set up no enforcement method for Section 7A, and though National Labor Boards were created first by President Roosevelt and then by congressional resolution, these were largely powerless.

To preserve the gains of Section 7A and strengthen the machinery, Congress in 1935 passed the Wagner National Labor Relations Act. This set forth the right of Labor to bargain collectively and created the National Labor Relations Board (NLRB) to enforce this right. The act used two means to create and preserve collective bargaining. (1) It set up machinery under the NLRB to choose and certify labor unions as bargaining agents. The board was to supervise elections in industrial units and certify the winners of these elections to be the legal bargaining agents for the workers in the units. (2) The act created a set of rules concerning such matters as unfair labor practices on the part of employers. The rules concerning these practices, defined as attempts by employers to discourage bargaining, to harm unions, or to threaten union members, were also to be enforced by the NLRB, subject to judicial review.

In 1947, after twelve years of operating experience under the Wagner Act, the Taft-Hartley Act amended the law to change the rules, making them more proemployer. Taft-Hartley, for example, added a list of unfair union practices to the employer practices, but it preserved the structure of the right to bargain. In 1959, the Landrum-Griffin Act amended the basic National Labor Relations Act in a new way by creating a set of rules governing the internal workings of unions. These three laws, then, which constitute the National Labor Relations Act (NLRA) as amended, form the basis of the public labor relations policies of the United States.

The original NLRA was an attempt to correct one of the two basic drawbacks to the free market system discussed above, its tendency to distribute its rewards so unequally as to be considered inequitable. As noted above, the onset of the Depression brought with it the realization that in fact the uncontrolled economic system had been working inequitably. The NLRA's attempt to correct the inequities can be looked at in two ways. (1) Foremost, in the minds of its authors, the act was a broad-based attempt to set the conditions for equity by helping people do for themselves rather than using legislation or administration to hand down a set of rules of equity. (2) However, the act did write rules: It set up a system of industrial jurisprudence in which the unfair practices and other rules of the act might be considered analogous to the U.S. Constitution, the Bill of Rights in particular, and the rulings of the NLRB as supported or reinterpreted by the courts, analogous to the body of Supreme Court decisions interpreting the Constitution.

For the most part, the system of jurisprudence was intended as an attempt to enforce the right of bargaining rather than to set up a legal system separating the fair from the unfair in employment relationships or to enforce equity by law. This marked a departure from much of the body of earlier labor law. Through the nineteenth century, and into the twentieth, the courts had tended to use the rules of equity and common law to regulate labor relations, and in doing so, they regulated according to their interpretation of the existing standards of fairness. Even before the New Deal, these rulings were amended legislatively, but Section 7A of the NIRA and the NLRA marked the first intentional departure away from court rulings on fair labor relations and toward setting up a system which it was hoped would create fair relations internally through the bargaining process. The departure was not complete because the system of jurisprudence under the NLRA necessarily takes on some aspects of an imposed system of equity; ultimately the board and the courts do end up ruling on what is fair, and the later amendments to the law have stressed this equity aspect. The Landrum-Griffin Act, in particular, was devoted entirely to the equities of a union versus the individuals who make up its membership.

It is useful therefore to compare the effectiveness of the system of rules and jurisprudence with the effectiveness of the workings of collective bargaining created by the system. The rules under the NLRA have covered a very wide area. Even in setting up collective bargaining initially (determining whom it is the workers want to represent them), a whole set of rules and methods has been necessary. The question of defining the unit within which a bargaining election should be held, for example, is a crucial one. By the early NLRB stress on plantwide bargaining units in many industries rather than elections among the members of a particular craft skill, for example, the Board made possible the development of mass industrial unionism among semiskilled and unskilled workers and the concomitant birth of the CIO. When to hold an election was also important. During the early days of the Wagner Act (and to some extent even today) it was difficult enough to get workers into a union in the face of determined employer opposition. Consequently the timing of the election so that employee willingness to vote "yes" on the union was at a peak became rather important to the unions. Even the interpretation of the results required NLRB discretion; where two unions were competing and the threeway vote among the two and no union at all was split so that no viewpoint had a majority, the Board interpreted the results to require a runoff between the leading union and no union.

The unfair practices set up by the Wagner Act required even more interpretation. These unfair employer practices were: (1) to interfere with employees attempting to exercise their right to bargain; (2) to attempt to set up a company union; (3) to use discrimination in hiring, firing, or other working conditions to encourage or discourage union membership; (4) to fire or discriminate against an employee who filed charges under the NLRA; and (5) to refuse to bargain collectively with the chosen union. The Taft-Hartley Act adjusted these practices; notably it added a list of unfair union practices somewhat parallel to the employer list. The Taft-Hartley Act also added to the jurisprudential aspects of the law by defining legitimate methods for unions and employers engaged in exerting bargaining pressure on one another. For example, the Taft-Hartley Act outlawed the secondary boycott, by which unions had attempted to pressure employers by striking customers of these employers; it expanded employer rights by allowing the employer "free speech" in talking to his employees about union membership or contract terms. Under the Wagner Act, the NLRB had closely limited the employer's speech because of the fear of implied threats against the union.

The Taft-Hartley Act also limited union political activity by outlawing the expenditure of union funds raised through dues collection to attempt to affect the results of political elections. Most important in regard to expanding the scope of the system of jurisprudence as compared to bargaining, however, was that the Taft-Hartley Act wrote into law for the first time restrictions on the subjects for bargaining. The act outlawed collectively bargained agreement to a closed shop, for example. It set rules about welfare funds created through bargaining.

This was the first time under the NLRA that the written law itself had moved back into substantive equity by ruling certain kinds of substance inequitable, or equitable only under certain kinds of conditions. However, it was not the first time that such questions had been raised, since from the very beginning the question of proper subjects for bargaining had been one of the most controversial issues ruled on by the NLRB. When the Wagner Act imposed the duty on the employer to bargain in good faith with the union representing his employees, the interpretation of this was not so clear as it might have been. One commonsense interpretation, one that seems to be quoted by every participant in the controversy over the definition of "good faith bargaining," was that of Sen. David Walsh, the chairman of the Senate Committee on Education and Labor at the time the Wagner Act was written:

> When the employees have chosen their organization, when they have selected their representatives, all the bill proposes to do is to escort them to the door of the employer and say, "Here they are, the legal representatives of your employees." What happens behind those doors is not inquired into, and the bill does not seek to inquire into it.[26]

But the NLRB interpreted good faith as concerning not only the occurrences outside the bargaining room door, but also behind the door. The NLRB concerned itself deeply with the style of bargaining and the subjects on which employers had to be willing to bargain in order to demonstrate good faith. By defining subjects in particular, the Board brought substantive equity into the law. That employers had to bargain over pension systems, for example, seemed to imply that having a pension system with shared control by the union was a desirable outcome; the employer reiteration that he wished the pension system to be completely controlled by himself was considered outside the scope of good faith bargaining. Many authorities have attacked this aspect of the NLRB interpretation of the law; some have defended it. The point to be made here, however, is that it is extremely difficult to define the jurisprudential aspects of the NLRA. Designed to create an enforcing structure in which all the rules are to be set by private party bargaining, the jurisprudence also almost necessarily gets into questions of substantive equity. Indeed, the last set of amendments to the NLRA, the Landrum-Griffin Act, specifically got into substantive questions in regard to democracy in the unions.

In any case, the general point is that U.S. labor relations law has by no means been a complete success as a system of equity through jurisprudence. What is to be considered equitable has been a subject of great controversy for three and one-half decades; the law has been changed substantially two times, and withall, it is not clear that procedures under the law are any fairer than they would have been without the law. Or at least it is not clear that procedures under the law are fairer than they would have been under a much broader, less highly administered piece of legislation in which equity was worked out within the collective bargaining process. Interpretation of rules by public officials works little better there than in the case of public assistance or the draft.

What is clear, however, is that, in contrast to the system of jurisprudence as such, the economic and political forces let loose and encouraged by the Wagner Act have made a vast difference in U.S. life since 1935. Just as modern industry might well be impossible without the corporate form of organization, it may be that modern egalitarian American society would be impossible without the growth of unionism consequent on passage of the Wagner Act. The growth of unionism may not require such legislation at all times and at all places; it has grown in the United Kingdom, for example, with virtually no law at all. But a strong argument can be made that whatever is needed to encourage unionism (and in the United States the Wagner Act was needed), unions themselves are a necessary ingredient in what has transpired in this and other free countries during the last thirty-five years.

The United States is different today economically, politically, and socially from what it would have been without strong trade unions. Economically, the case is somewhat difficult to make by use of aggregate statistics. Employees' share of national income has not increased significantly over time, for example, but this proves little. It has been difficult, for instance, to separate the effects of unionism on unionized workers from those on non-unionized workers; the former have gained relatively but this may have been at the expense of nonunion workers rather than profit receivers. More important is the possibility that even though the share of employees in the national income has been relatively constant over the long run because the real workings of the system tend to compensate for initial union gains, the effect of unions on aggregate economic growth as well as labor's share has resulted in a large increase of the absolute standard of living of American workers. Instead of the economy settling down to a lower growth pattern, constant union pressure, forcing management to search for cost-cutting economies that might compensate for union wage gains, together with rapid growth of consumer markets due to union-initiated wage gains in mass industries, seem to have pushed the system to more rapid growth than would otherwise have been the case. The union pressures and the mass markets have certainly been inflationary factors; low levels of unemployment have been obtainable only at a higher price in inflation than would otherwise have been possible. But the pressures also have very likely impelled investment and business growth through the management effort to cut costs by finding substitutes for expensive labor, and they have induced business growth by the guarantee of a mass market.

In addition, outside of the direct wage bargain, unions have forced other economic changes that have made the United States look quite different from what it otherwise would have been. The union effect on working conditions has been substantial. For better or for worse, unions have cut down piecework and speedups. Seniority and other devices have provided a sense of security not previously available. Union pressure for pensions obtained through collective bargaining has helped restructure the lives of retirees. And so forth.

The political change induced by the labor unions in the United States can be seen even more clearly than the economic change. Since the mid-1930s, the labor movement has become a major political power. In terms of membership, in terms of funds available for political support (voluntary collections rather than dues, in order to obey the Taft-Hartley law), in terms of cadres of union employees and members willing to work politically, the union growth encouraged by the Wagner Act has made for a far different political balance in the United States than otherwise would have been the case. It is obvious that during recent years John Kennedy would not have been elected President without the unions; his victory was so close that every factor contributing to it was crucial. Union power in the 1968 election came close to doing the impossible by almost electing Hubert Humphrey; what was even more impressive during 1968 was the evident effect of union organizations in weaning their members away from a fear-induced affinity for George Wallace. Most fundamental, however, has been the day-to-day work of unions in electing congressmen and state and local legislators amenable to what they believe to be the interest of their members. The basic progressive thrust of American legislation has been largely due to the Wagner Act. It is notable that even though race and other fears have tended to deflect this thrust somewhat in recent years on some issues, the direction is truer than ever in regard to issues like social insurance that continue to affect the now middle-class membership of labor unions.

Finally, the effect of the Wagner Act encouragement of labor unions on the social fabric of the United States has been substantial. Federal protection and encouragement of collective bargaining has given American workers a feeling of control over their own destiny—on and off the job—and by doing so has made them part of the "system." The alternative may well have been alienation and revolt; thus, the effect of bringing workers into the system may have been the most crucial of all.

The overall point, then, is that though the NLRA and its various amendments have been irregular in their effects on equity through jurisprudence, the forces loosed by the laws have clearly had a major impact. By adding a new vector to the complex set of power relationships affecting American economic, political, and social life, the direction of movement of the entire system has been changed. If one's value system includes the belief that equity requires greater consideration of the rights of workers than was given during the 1920s, the change has been favorable. Specifically, it has been more favorable than could have been expected from a complete legislative and administrative system setting up public machinery for fixing wages, conditions of work, and equities.

Indeed, in the view of some value systems, the Wagner Act overshot its mark by giving too much power to labor and the purpose of the Taft-Hartley Act was to correct the balance of forces, weighting it somewhat more toward management. If the effect of the Wagner Act was more noticeable for the forces it loosed than for its direct effect on equity, the corrective of Taft-Hartley is more noticeable for the counterforces loosed than for the corrections to inequity. After the passage of Taft-Hartley, for example, a noticeable slowdown in union growth took place, and though this was the result of many factors in addition to Taft-Hartley, many specific cases can be pointed out in which the change in the law was the operative force. Particularly in the South, where union organization came almost to a dead halt, a major reason was the slowing down of the certifying system and the system of correcting unfair practices. The Taft-Hartley Act vastly increased the ability of the employer to delay action, and this delay in turn made it far more difficult for unions to organize plants, to keep the organization intact under employer pressures no longer clearly illegal as under the Wagner Act, and ultimately to win bargaining elections. In the minds of at least some backers of the Taft-Hartley Act, this was just the point.

The NLRA thus has released forces of self-interest that have made a substantial difference in American life. But, to finish this section near where it began, the question may be asked why the NLRA released forces that, working on the price of labor as well as other aspects of the conditions of work, had such major effects, whereas the NRA failed to release such forces to affect the prices of the goods sold by business. NRA, after all, did try to provide power to trade associations of business, in many ways analogous to labor unions. The complete answer is, of course, complex, and must include constitutional and other legal questions as well as referring to the attitudes of the early New Deal period, which were far more prolabor than probusiness. But the key difference between NLRA and NRA is not these; it lies in the uses made of the power released. The labor unionism released by NLRA worked, even on the price of labor, because unions by and large represented the self-interest of all their members and used their power for bargaining in an adversary procedure against employers; there was no union-undermining tradition for individual workers to compete for jobs by cutting wages. The trade associationism released by NRA failed in its attempts at price fixing because the tradition and economic basis of competition in product markets led to chiseling, to cutting below the set prices; self-interest guided so many businessmen to cut prices in order to gain larger shares of the market that the system broke down. Indeed, when analogous situations sometimes arose in the labor market (unions representing both unskilled and skilled workers, for example), the resultant tensions sometimes came close to destroying the unions. What it comes to is that adversary advocacy and bargaining work better than attempted cooperation of naturally opposed interests.

Community Action

During the last few years the parallel has frequently been drawn between the workings of the labor movement, particularly during the 1930s, and the Community Action Program of the 1960s. In fact, the analogy is an interesting one and not too strained.

The Economic Opportunity Act of 1964, which created the

Office of Economic Opportunity (OEO) and began the officially designated War on Poverty, created the Community Action Program as a major portion of the antipoverty effort. Community Action was to be a program of federal funding of local public and private nonprofit groups for locally planned and locally carried out antipoverty programs. In practice, most of the funding went to private nonprofit organizations specifically set up for the purpose, a fact that is important for the later discussion, as is the freedom of these organizations to design programs across a broad range of functions and types.

Daniel P. Moynihan has categorized four basic lines of thought that fed into the creation of the Community Action Program in 1964. These are community action as careful, detailed local planning, an idea Moynihan attributes to the federal Bureau of the Budget; as power confrontation by the poverty community with the majority community, which he traces back to the theories of Saul Alinsky; as delivering benefits to the poor from the better-off, attributed to Sargent Shriver; and, politically as a largely untapped vein of votes.[27] Moynihan argues that these four streams are not compatible, a somewhat questionable contention, but he is certainly correct that all four existed, at least at first. The last two, however, soon disappeared as operational considerations. The Peace Corps concept remained relevant to certain specific programs, such as Head Start, but these programs moved outside of the locally controlled core of Community Action to a great extent. The votes were not so easy to mine as may have appeared to some, and in retrospect any politician who went into Community Action during 1964–1965 with the thought of getting votes, must have become sorely disappointed indeed by 1966. The other two streams of thought, the planning ideas of the Budget Bureau and the confrontation concept, however, have a good deal of parallelism to the jurisprudential and the force-releasing aspects of the Wagner Act and are useful to consider in this light.

The first thing to be said about local planning of Community Action is that such planning in the sense of meaningful self-conscious laying out of a course that is likely to be followed hardly ever took place, nor did the federal government demand it of the communities. True, a "plan" was required in local applications for federal grants, but what was presented as a plan was seldom much more than a list of widely disparate projects, ranging from manpower training to household sewing, each with a separate rationale. Such lists were readily accepted by the federal officials if the individual projects seemed to meet the requirements. The lists were seldom based on anything that a planner would call a plan. Occasionally, there were surveys, studies, and so forth, but even when these were present, their relationships to the grant application were obscure.

Four reasons for this lack of planning are obvious in the clear light of hindsight:

1. Careful planning was simply not compatible with getting the dollars out fast, and getting the dollars out fast was the prime desideratum of both federal officials and local grantees. From OEO Director Sargent Shriver on down, they were all activists. The locals were not about to wait around to do a careful plan; the federal officials were not about to turn down a grant application from a deserving community group because it contained no such plan.

2. It was extremely difficult to do such planning. This may be illustrated by the results of several years of attempts within the OEO to create some sort of manual to aid local groups in planning. At least three such separate attempts were made; none succeeded. The reason was that the simplest set of rules that could be prepared at the federal level and still conceivably lead to meaningful planning was still far more complex than all but the most sophisticated communities could possibly utilize. The science or art of comprehensive planning simply had not reached local community groups. Perhaps, as contended throughout this book, this science is not really available at all.

3. Funds at the local level were distributed among deserving agencies and projects by a political process of bargaining: so much for you, so much for me. Such planners as were available to local groups had not reached a level of sophistication or

power that brought them directly into the bargaining sphere. They were thus largely irrelevant to the process of distributing funds under Community Action grants.

4. Finally, not a direct cause of lack of planning, but related, is the fact that the hoped-for Community Action function of coordinating local poverty programs turned out to be politically impossible in virtually all jurisdictions. Community Action Agencies were dropped into the midst of powerful existing groups—boards of education, welfare authorities, city divisions, and so forth—and these agencies did not particularly care to be coordinated by a new, small, federally sponsored upstart. They had the power to get the money and avoid the coordination. Nor, in many cases, did local private nonprofit Community Action groups want to work with city hall.

For all these reasons, those people in the Budget Bureau and elsewhere who stressed planning felt after a few years that Community Action was a dead failure because of the failure of its planning. But just as the NLRA can be considered questionable on its effectiveness as a system of jurisprudence but successful in unleashing forces that led to a new balance of equity, the Community Action failure in planning still allowed a very marked degree of success in unleashing forces, particularly within the urban complexes of the United States. (Success here must be defined, however, in relation to a set of values that defines the outcomes discussed below as successful. Many would throw doubt on these definitions, as some would throw doubts on the values by which collective bargaining can be termed successful.)

The forces released were related to those Moynihan refers to when he talks of confrontation, though the confrontation characterization is not entirely accurate. Community Action as the release of forces did have some antecedents in the theories and experimental attempts at radical confrontation. The major experiment of this sort was Mobilization for Youth, a pre-War on Poverty community action program funded by the Ford Foundation Gray Areas project. But by the beginning of the federal Community Action Program, the confrontation aspects of Mobilization for Youth had provided so much controversy that they threw doubt on the confrontation theories themselves, and except for a few special projects, radical confrontation was not the theme of Community Action under the federal program.

Indeed, behind the familiar language, "Maximum feasible participation of the residents of the areas and members of the target groups affected," were not only the confrontation ideas but also (as Moynihan also points out) [28] the desire to preserve civil rights in the South, and just plain citizen participation as a good democratic ideal. During the first year of the War on Poverty, the radical end of the spectrum of theories of local group and individual action was occasionally pushed by OEO, but under political pressures from the White House and for other reasons, what radical push existed was modified. By 1968, James Sundquist and David Davis were able to categorize three types of Community Action Agencies:

1. The innocuous ones, found mainly in smaller communities. They were the ones of whom it was said, "Oh, they're all right; they're not doing much." That type of CAA had found its place in the cluster of social agencies in its community, as another specialized organization quietly administering a few programs designed in Washington. Sponsored initially by the power structure, it had not challenged the institutions and leadership of that structure.

2. The respected ones—those that were aggressive, even militant, but with a quality of leadership and administrative competence to match. The respect was accorded not willingly but grudgingly, usually not because of their achievements but because of their political strength, which rested upon the mobilization of the poor. And they stood apart from, and in a position of confrontation with, the established institutions of their communities.

3. The outcasts—those that had not been able to match their militancy with a leadership and competence that compelled respect. They were effectively contained, left to administer the programs financed from Washington but otherwise ignored or even shunned.[29]

This was not the pattern expressed by the planners of the legislation or the administrators, but was the result of release of forces by Community Action.

This course of Community Action had two major results,

one internal to the poverty communities represented by the Community Action Agencies, and an external one concerning their relationships with the larger communities of which they were a part.[30]

The internal result is parallel to the social aspects of the Wagner Act in giving workers a degree of control over their own destinies. Though most of the poor in the United States are not members of racial or ethnic minorities, the most difficult problems of poverty are those associated with race, ghettos, or slums. Before the onset of Community Action in 1964–1965, in addition to all the other problems inherent in poverty, slums, particularly black ghettos, were disorganized. They had no self-help institutions whereby the more successful members of the group could help the less successful; in fact, they had few institutions of any kind. The old churches up from the South were losing their grip on urban black populations, and the civil rights organizations active during the 1950s and early 1960s cut only into the Negro middle class, not into the low-level mass. And as a result of this disorganization combined with poverty, the atmosphere in the ghetto was one of helplessness, sureness of failure, no handholds to get up or out. The ghetto poor were apathetic and alienated from society. In this, the black ghetto of 1960 differed from earlier ethnic ghettos in the United States: the Jews had their Workers Alliances, the Irish their saloon-based political organizations, the Italians their old-village societies; each of these helped raise the group as a whole, as well as individuals within it. For reasons having to do with the history of slavery and all the rest, Negroes had nothing similar.

Community Action changed this, not singlehandedly, but as a major factor in the change. In contrast to the early 1960s, the ghettos are now characterized by a rich profusion of social, political, and economic organizations, ranging from the militant to the moderate, and jostling up against one another in an active internal institutional political life. Where there were few institutions earlier, now the problem, if it is a problem, is the competition of what may be too many. Much of the initial impetus and many of the first nuclei for these institutions were Community Action organizations of one sort or another. And, in an analogy to the social effects of the growth of unionism during the 1930s, the organizational life is turning ghetto dwellers away from alienation. Indeed, though it is not always clear when one looks at some of the militant organizations in the ghettos, organizational life may even be turning the ghettoes away from revolt.

If the growth of the internal life within the ghetto may be considered parallel to the social effects of the union movement, the change in the external relations of the ghetto with the rest of the community is parallel to the political and economic bargaining effects of the early growth of trade unionism. Around the new institutional nuclei within the ghetto gathered political forces powerful enough to make the ghetto listened to in the wider community. The new institutions began to bargain for the ghetto, particularly in the coalition middle-way model of Sundquist and Davis. And this fact of bargaining, where previously the blacks and the ghetto could largely be ignored in most communities, made for major real differences in the way urban institutions treated the ghetto residents. Before Community Action, public employment offices were downtown and out of reach; after Community Action, they set up offices in the ghetto. Before Community Action, boards of education tended to ignore the problems of ghetto schools; now if anything, they spend most of their time on these problems. Before Community Action, welfare agencies were cold and bureaucratic; they still are but less so. Like the labor union phenomenon, community action (lower-case intended, since the forms may change) has become a permanent political force to be contended with, particularly in urban communities and to a lesser extent in national politics. This is true even though the power of the organization of the poor is less than that of the unions and will always be less simply because the relative numbers are less; this fact is important to keep in mind for any direct comparison of the effectiveness of collective bargaining and community action.

In any case, the relevant point to be made here is similar to that on collective bargaining. The elaborate planning structure is questionable in its direct effectiveness: In the case of collective bargaining, the elaborate structure of jurisprudence may be a necessary protection for carrying out such bargaining. (Or at least it may have been so initially during the 1930s, though now the controversy over the meaning of the requirement for "bargaining in good faith" on a variety of subjects casts doubts on the importance of the structural elaborateness.) In the case of Community Action, the elaborate structure and philosophy of planning may have been useful for a few years as a cover (a "social myth") that was relatively acceptable to the majority of the political forces of the country while in fact the real function of Community Action was not planning but the release of forces to represent minorities. In both cases, however, the important result was the unleashing or promoting of bargaining forces that in the case of the labor movement made for fundamental changes in our society and economy, and in the case of Community Action may be making for such changes as well. Specifically, these bargaining mechanisms are the first in the entire set of mechanisms looked at in this chapter that seem to be relatively effective in correcting the inequities inherent in an otherwise well-functioning economic system.

Notes

1. *The New York Times,* July 10, 1969, p. 1.
2. Figures derived from U.S. Internal Revenue Service, Statistics of Income for 1965 and 1966 (Washington, D.C.: Government Printing Office, 1968), tables 24 and 37.
3. Joseph A. Pechman, *Federal Tax Policy* (Washington, D.C.: The Brookings Institution, 1966), tables C–10, p. 284.
4. Jens P. Jensen, *Property Taxation in the United States* (Chicago: University of Chicago Press, 1931) as quoted in Dick Netzer, *Economics of the Property Tax* (Washington, D.C.: The Brookings Institution, 1966).
5. Dick Netzer, *Economics of the Property Tax,* table 7–5, p. 190.
6. *Ibid.,* table 3–10, p. 55.
7. *Ibid.,* pp. 56–57.
8. Perry Prentice, "Better Assessments for Better Cities," *Nation's Cities,* May 1970, p. 20.
9. *Ibid.,* pp. 35–39.

10. *The Report of the President's Commission on an All-Volunteer Armed Force* (Washington, D.C.: Government Printing Office, 1970), p. 148.

11. *Ibid.,* appendix A.

12. For a more extended discussion, see Robert A. Levine, *The Poor Ye Need Not Have with You: Lessons from the War on Poverty* (Cambridge: M.I.T. Press, 1970), pp. 183–186.

13. This is discussed in more detail in Levine, pp. 132–143.

14. Arthur M. Schlesinger, Jr., *The Coming of the New Deal* (Boston: Houghton Mifflin, 1958), p. 126.

15. *Ibid.,* p. 159.

16. *Ibid.,* p. 121.

17. The impossibility of substituting a pure peacetime system is pointed out even by those economists who argue for movement in the direction of a price system. See Tibor Scitovsky, Edward Shaw, and Lorie Tarshis, *Mobilizing Resources for War* (New York: McGraw-Hill, 1951), esp. pp. 135–139.

18. See David Novick, Melvin Anshen, and W. C. Truppner, *Wartime Production Controls* (New York: Columbia University Press, 1949), pp. 198 ff.

19. *Ibid.,* p. 192.

20. *Ibid.,* pp. 370–371.

21. William L. Slayton, "The Operation and Achievements of the Urban Renewal Program," in James Q. Wilson, ed., *Urban Renewal* (Cambridge: M.I.T. Press, 1966), p. 192.

22. Martin Anderson, "The Federal Bulldozer" in Wilson, ed., *Urban Renewal,* p. 495.

23. *Ibid.,* p. 506.

24. Robert P. Groberg, "Urban Renewal Realistically Reappraised" in Wilson, ed., *Urban Renewal,* p. 510.

25. William G. Grigsby, "A General Strategy for Urban Renewal" in Wilson, ed., *Urban Renewal,* p. 660.

26. Senator David Walsh, *Congressional Record,* 79th Congress (Washington, D.C.: GPO, 1935), pp. 1659–1660.

27. Daniel P. Moynihan, "What Is Community Action?" *The Public Interest,* No. 5, Fall 1966, pp. 3–8.

28. *Ibid.*

29. James L. Sundquist, with the collaboration of David W. Davis, *Making Federalism Work* (Washington, D.C.: The Brookings Institution, 1969), p. 47.

30. For a fuller discussion, see Levine, *The Poor Ye Need Not Have with You.*

4

Cases in Point: Military Policy and Planning

FORMAL MILITARY PLANNING has a far longer history than most of the planning discussed in the previous chapter. For this reason a terminology has been built up over the years, but with the changes in style of warfare over the past several decades there has come a weakening of this language, leading to some semantic problems. Most of these revolve around the words "strategic" and "tactical." "Strategic" generally connotes something big and long run; "tactical," something small and short run. But bigness has proliferated over so many dimensions that the words have varied in definition. In this study the word "strategic" is used to mean a kind of war or planning for war in which the objective of military operations is, at a minimum, a fundamental change in world power relationships, at a maximum, national survival; "tactical" is anything less.

These definitions fit well the connotations of bigness and littleness. Unfortunately, however, they leave undefined some other important distinctions that also have bigness and littleness connotations and sometimes are fit into the strategic-tactical dichotomy. One way to put this additional distinction that crosses the strategic-tactical one is to distinguish between force planning and operational planning, between hardware and its utilization. Hardware takes a long time to plan. The force-operational distinction thus picks up the long-run versus short-run dichotomy just as the strategic-tactical distinction picks up the difference between bigness and littleness. This is not completely satisfactory, however, because force planning is not the only kind of long-run planning. Doctrine for the use of force (the general and sometimes specific philosophy of such use) is also long-run planning, and doctrine for force use is frequently as difficult to change quickly as are the forces themselves. The distinction drawn here, therefore, is between force and doctrine planning on the one hand and operational planning on the other. The first of these is similar to the kind of planning that has been treated in the domestic context thus far; the other has fewer domestic analogs.

Force and doctrine planning, then, involve the layout of courses of future actions, these actions being the purchase of hardware, the recruiting and training of men, their organizational structure, and their deployment. This is the force planning side; the doctrine side involves the laying out in advance of the techniques and tactics by which these forces will be utilized. These are both long-run activities. While doctrine might in principle be flexible in the short run, it seldom is. Force and doctrine planning have their domestic parallel in the adoption by the War Production Board of the Controlled Materials Plan discussed above, to take one example.

Operational planning is also carried out in advance—all planning is by definition carried out in advance—but operational planning is at least supposed to be quite flexible. As the conditions under which an operation (for example, a Marine landing in Vietnam) is carried out change, the plans are supposed to change too. As the intermediate steps of the plan unfold differently from the way that was initially assumed (for example, less enemy resistance than expected), the plan also should change quickly. A domestic parallel to this planning might be the specific application of the Controlled Materials Plan to copper used in wiring radars during World War II. What is interesting for this study in the military as well as the civilian context is more the conditions for carrying out successful operational planning, conditions that are largely based on force and doctrine plans, than the details of operational planning itself.

Flexible operational plans are laid out and frequently they work. The strategic operational plans that took the allied forces in World War II from D-Day through VE-Day were changed many times to take advantage of opportunity as in the Normandy breakthrough, or to prevent disaster as in the Bulge. Tactical operating plans were changed even more frequently. Sometimes operational plans thought flexible do not work. The best example of this, Vietnam, is taken up in some detail below. And in one case (and perhaps only one), operational plans are not flexible at all. The plans for the carrying out of strategic nuclear war, though they offer many options in targets and patterns, must be presumed to be inflexible once the option has been chosen and gone beyond the point of no return. (The reference here might as well be *Dr. Strangelove.*)

This chapter, then, is primarily about long-run military planning, the planning of forces and doctrine. The discussion cuts across strategic and tactical planning; it also cuts across planning by civilians and planning by military men, another important distinction. For the most part civilian planning is stressed because that is most parallel to the long-run domestic planning of the previous chapter. But in the case of Vietnam, the interplay of military and civilian planning is in itself instructive.

And finally as a point of introduction, all the military planning discussed in this chapter must be distinguished from the domestic planning of the last on one major conceptual point, the definition of waste. Military operations are sometimes (but not always) considered wasteful if, for example, the first three efforts fail but the fourth one works. But they are hardly ever considered wasteful if the first works and the hardware purchased for the second, third, and fourth is not used. Military planning—both for forces and doctrine—ordinarily contains deliberately built-in redundancy. If one try does not work, try again. This is particularly true in the case of the strategic planning discussed in the next section, but redundancy pervades military planning.

And whereas some military planning sometimes succeeds by use of redundancy, such redundancy is almost never available to domestic social programs, where it would be shunned as pure waste. This is important to keep in mind, as it relates to the sometimes-heard contention that the trouble with social programs is that they do not use the kind of planning done for military (or space) efforts. The different concept of waste makes a big difference. And even so, as discussed below, most military planning works as poorly as most civilian planning anyhow, and for similar reasons.

Strategic Warfare and Strategic Planning

The word "strategic" has been defined above to cover those military actions whose objective is, at a minimum, a fundamental change in world power relationships, at a maximum, national survival. In other words, it is very important that strategic planning succeed. Because of this importance, the different nature of the military concept of waste, discussed above, is greatly magnified. And when the objective of the planning is clear and relatively simple, as it frequently is in strategic cases (for example, deterring massive Soviet nuclear attack), the strategic military planning and operations considered in this section begin to look quite different from the planning and operations in any of the domestic cases discussed in the last chapter.

Specifically, planning, in the sense of laying out a single course for future actions, becomes far less important in these cases because we are willing to try many alternative courses simultaneously. The courses that do not work or are not needed are not considered waste, which they would have been in the cases of the previous chapter. Under these conditions, strategic plans—strategic force plans—are very likely to succeed in the sense of meeting the reasonable expectations of the planners. But they succeed not because of good planning, but because if we try everything, it seems statistically likely that something is going to work.

Looking at the strategic force planning of World War II, for example, it is certainly not the case that waste recognized as such did not exist during the war. It existed pervasively, and it was notably exposed by Senator Harry S. Truman's investigating committee, the inquiries of which were considered important enough to make Truman Vice President of the United States. But nobody took this recognized kind of waste as a reason for failing to prosecute the war vigorously or for even running it differently. It was considered a necessary cost of reaching a crucial objective, and again this is quite different from any ordinary domestic operation.

But beyond the kind of waste recognized as such, the importance of prosecuting the war led to the kind of planning that in any other context would have been considered wasteful in the extreme. All sorts of examples might be cited, but perhaps the best comes from the development of nuclear weapons in the Manhattan Project. In many ways this development was the most critical of the war (at least while it seemed that we were racing the Germans), and this criticality determined the way things were done. Even with the criticality, however, the approach was rather startling. According to Stephane Groueff, when it was determined in 1942 that there were five ways, all untested, of producing nuclear material:

> The pressure to make a decision was undeniably great. "The Germans are at present probably far ahead of us," Arthur Compton pointed out. "They started their program vigorously in 1939, but ours was not undertaken with similar vigor until 1941." Conant agreed: "If the new weapon is going to be the determining factor in the war, then there is a desperate need for speed. Three months' delay might be disastrous."
> At this point the scientists abandoned their usual method of inquiry. Logically the task would be selecting the best of five methods. The problem, however, was no longer which would be the best —the success of each was equally improbable—but which would be the *fastest*. Unfortunately, there was no way of predicting this, nor was there any time for guessing wrong and trying all over again. The S-1 Committee then made one of the boldest decisions of the entire war. Since the members were unable to select one method over the others, they agreed that *all* five methods should be tried simultaneously. Such a program would entail the building of five large-scale plants such as had never been seen or even thought of before, those equipment and technological processes would have to be invented and developed from scratch. Whole new industries would have to be created in a colossal scientific and technological adventure of incalculable consequences for the nation.[1]

This kind of solution takes care of most of the problems of planning and management. It is not typically available for most cases. Domestic programs do sometimes carry out experimentation, but never by carrying out each alternative full scale.

A different sort of example from World War II comes from the strategic bombing of Germany. Burton Klein points out:

> Based on a detailed examination of losses in the damaged industries, it was the conclusion of the United States Strategic Bombing Survey that prior to mid-1943, neither the British nor the U.S. attacks had a significant effect on military output as a whole; that in the second half of 1943 and the first half of 1944 they caused losses of some 5 and 10 percent respectively.
> The expected effects of the attacks were, of course, much greater.[2]

The point here is not that the planning of the strategic bombing was necessarily bad, but rather that during wartime it is possible to try a lot of things on speculation. The strategic bombing of Germany might be considered a large-scale experiment, the dream of social program makers; in this case, the experiment failed in significantly reducing the German war potential. It was not considered waste, and indeed much was learned that was applicable to nuclear planning efforts.

The final example from World War II is one where the real waste seems clearer, though I do not know of any discussions of it. World War II was supposed to have marked the triumph of the aircraft carrier over the battleship in the U.S. Navy. Four battleships of the Missouri class were begun just before the war and completed during the war. Though these were of major assistance during the many landings of the Pacific war, they seemed to provide little rationale for further enlargement of the battleship fleet at a time when the war would surely be over. Nonetheless, in December 1944, the U.S.S. Kentucky was begun and in January 1945 the U.S.S. Illinois. This was at a time when the end of the war was in sight, well after the Normandy invasion and clearly too late for the ships to participate in the invasion of Japan, which was then thought to be necessary. Even so, neither ship was cancelled until after the war had ended, and at that time, they were roughly two-thirds completed, which means that each had already cost the greater part of $100 million. It seems clear that by the standards applied to domestic programs and even by the standards applied since 1945 to military programs, these costs were clearly unjustified and came close to pure waste. Nonetheless, they were not questioned at the time, nor, so far as I can find out, subsequently.[3]

The same kinds of standards applied to expenditures during World War II have also been applied to the strategy of nuclear deterrence since then. What has been considered necessary to make very sure that the Soviets would be deterred from attacking the United States has been done and done in a way applicable only to a policy with a crucially important and relatively clearcut objective, deterring nuclear attack on the United States. It is of course nonsense to say that the money spent in deterrence has been wasted because the expensive weapon systems were never used in anger. The B-36 and the B-47 and the Thor and Jupiter missiles have been phased out without use, and one can only be thankful for this.

Rather than simple waste, the situation has been similar to that of World War II in which we were willing to try a wide variety of weapons and tactics, and the result has been an elaborate system of deterrent weapons and defenses of deterrent weapons put together with a redundancy similar to that of aircraft safety systems. A key contribution to the debate that led to this solution was that of Albert Wohlstetter in 1959. It is worth quoting at length because it is an excellent example of the kind of reasoning behind strategic (and much other military) planning.

Deterrence . . . , is not automatic. While feasible, it will be much harder to achieve in the 1960s than is generally believed. One of the most disturbing features of current opinion is the underestimation of this difficulty. This is due partly to a misconstruction of the technological race as a problem in matching striking forces, partly to a wishful analysis of the Soviet ability to strike first. . . .

One intelligent commentator, Richard Rovere, recently expressed the common view: "If the Russians had ten thousand warheads and a missile for each, and we had ten hydrogen bombs and ten obsolete bombers, . . . aggression would still be a folly that would appeal only to an insane adventurer." Mr. Rovere's example is plausible because it assumes implicitly that the defender's hydrogen bombs will with certainty be visited on the aggressor; then the damage done by the ten bombs seems terrible enough for deterrence, and any more would be simply redundant. This is the basis for the common view. . . .

Some of the complexities can be suggested by referring to the successive obstacles to be hurdled by any system providing a capability to strike second, that is, to strike back. Such deterrent systems must have (a) a stable, "steady-state" peacetime operation within feasible budgets (besides the logistic and operational costs there are, for example, problems of false alarms and accidents). They must have also the ability (b) to survive enemy attacks, (c) to make and communicate the decision to retaliate, (d) to reach enemy territory with fuel enough to complete their mission, (e) to penetrate enemy active defenses, that is, fighters and surface-to-air missiles, and (f) to destroy the target in spite of any "passive" civil defense in the form of dispersal or protective construction or evacuation of the target itself. . . .

In counteracting the general optimism as to the ease and, in fact, the inevitability of deterrence, I should like to avoid creating the extreme opposite impression. Deterrence demands hard, continuing, intelligent work, but it can be achieved. The job of deterring rational attack by guaranteeing great damage to an aggressor is, for example, very much less difficult than erecting a nearly airtight defense of cities in the face of full-scale thermonuclear surprise attack. Protecting manned bombers and missiles is much easier because they may be dispersed, sheltered or kept mobile, and they can respond to warning with greater speed. Mixtures of these and other defenses with complementary strengths can preserve a powerful remainder after attack. Obviously not all our bombers and missiles need to survive in order to fulfill their mission. To preserve the majority of our cities intact in the face of surprise attack is immensely more difficult, if not impossible. . . . Deterrence, however, provided we work at it, is feasible, and, what is more, it is a crucial objective of national policy.

What can be said, then, as to whether general war is unlikely? Would not a general thermonuclear war mean "extinction" for the aggressor as well as the defender? "Extinction" is a state that badly needs analysis. Russian casualties in World War II were more than 2,000,000. Yet Russia recovered extremely well from this catastrophe. There are several quite plausible circumstances in the future when the Russians might be quite confident of being able to limit damage to considerably less than this number—if they make sensible strategic choices and we do not. On the other hand, the risks of not striking might at some juncture appear very great to the Soviets, involving, for example, disastrous defeat in peripheral war, loss of key satellites with danger of revolt spreading—possibly to Russia itself—or fear of an attack by ourselves. Then, striking first, by surprise, would be the sensible choice for them, and from their point of view the smaller risk. . . .[4]

Most of Wohlstetter's recommendations were carried out during the early 1960s. They worked; there was no nuclear war during the 1960s. But was all the elaboration and cost necessary? Perhaps not, in the sense that there probably would not have been a nuclear war anyhow. The situation is illustrated by Figure 4–1 in which the horizontal axis shows the expected damage to the Soviet Union from American retaliation in case of a Soviet first strike on this country, and the vertical axis the

Damage to U.S.S.R. from U.S. retaliation
for Soviet first strike

Figure 4–1

probability of each level of damage. Wohlstetter's implication is that without a change in the policy he criticized in 1959, the likelihood of substantial damage from a U.S. retaliatory strike at the Soviet Union might be high, as in curve A, but this might not be high enough to deter a first Soviet attack under situations of extreme stress. Therefore, he argued, his recommended changes in posture were needed to shift the curve to B, where there would be only a small chance of less than very great damage to the Soviets. There might be only, say, a 10 percent chance of Soviet attack associated with curve A, but given the nature of that attack, 10 percent was too high for the United States to tolerate if we could by proper expenditures move the situation to curve B, which might imply, say, only a 1 percent chance of Soviet attack.

(In the United States itself during the early 1960s it was discovered that in fact this country was so strong relative to the Soviet Union that there was a pretty good chance for us to mount a first strike against them and escape scot-free. In other words, if Figure 4–1 were changed so that the horizontal axis read damage to the United States from Soviet retaliation in case of an American first strike, the real probability curve would be even tighter to the vertical axis than curve A in the figure, and the highest probability would be associated with almost no damage to this country. Some analysts [not Wohlstetter] argued on this basis for an aggressive U.S. policy but American decision-makers were not concerned with the bulk of the curve near the United States zero-damage point; they were concerned with the right tail of the curve which still illustrated some chance of things going wrong in a United States first strike with consequent great damage to our country. Possibly what might go wrong were the planners' calculations, and U.S. decision-makers, acting conservatively, were not willing to take seriously a policy with even that very small chance.)

Again, the acceptance of Wohlstetter's plea for protection and a multiplicity of systems was due to the crucial importance and relative simplicity of his objective of deterring Soviet attack. This led to the sort of planning and operations that made it possible to cover all possible contingencies rather than picking the most likely.

In any case, the strategic force planning of the United States typically has worked; we won World War II, we have not been attacked by the Soviet Union, and we have thus fulfilled the reasonable expectations of the planners. But this is true because the crucial and relatively simple nature of the objectives has led to what would be thought fantastic redundancy and waste by the criterion applied to domestic public programs. Indeed, the redundancy discussed here is only the smallest part of it. We have been discussing only the central planning of strategic forces. Yet we can be sure that the spirit of redundancy went all the way down the line in parts of these cases. The atom bomb manufacturer, the battleship builder, the strategic missile builder and operator did not want their components to be the weak links in the strategic chain. They too built in redundancy at each step, and the result was redundancy within redundancy. If the costs of making the atom bomb were multiplied by five by trying all five methods simultaneously, the ultimate costs were multiplied by many times five. If only one choice were made each time, and it were the right choice, costs would have been a very small fraction of what they actually were. At this point, one may object that "Of course, it is impossible to choose the right step each time." Yet this is close to the criterion of waste imposed on many nonmilitary programs.

NATO Planning

An example of what happens to military planning and operations when the peculiar urgencies surrounding strategic warfare are removed can be provided by the force and doctrine planning for the North Atlantic Treaty Organization (NATO) throughout the 1960s. NATO planning differs from strategic planning because (to the United States at least) the objectives are not so critically important as strategic deterrence and because these objectives are no longer clear and simple.

NATO's major objective may have been clear and simple in its early days during the 1950s (it was preventing or combating a massive Soviet attack on Western Europe) but as this Soviet threat faded through the 1960s, the objective became more conjectural. Further, though keeping Western Europe free of Soviet domination was a central objective of U.S. foreign and military policy, it was not perceived to be as important to the United States as preventing nuclear attack on this country. (At least the U.S. priority system was not so perceived by the European NATO members to whom their own freedom and continued existence was the supreme objective.) And finally, what was thought to be required for deterrence or defense against the Soviets was so expensive that these "requirements" were never taken seriously. As a result of this, NATO military planning throughout the 1960s was at least as unrealistic as the planning for any domestic program of the United States. NATO planning did not fail in the sense that it did not reach the reasonable expectations of the planners; it was so unrealistic that it never had much effect on operations at all.

NATO was created in 1949 as a paper organization; during the early 1950s it became the vehicle for central planning and unified control of Western European armed forces together with those U.S. and Canadian forces stationed in or committed to Europe. This centralized planning and unified control had two objectives: (1) the deterrence or defeat of a Soviet attack on Western Europe, an all-out attack by massive Russian and other Communist forces streaming across the Iron Curtain being the central event around which force and doctrine planning (as well as operational planning) revolved; (2) less explicit but almost as important, the placing of German forces under unified command. It was grudgingly conceded by the Western Europeans whose suffering at German hands was still very recent during the early 1950s that the Soviet threat made West Germany military power a necessity, but such German power was unacceptable under independent German command; hence, unified NATO command.

During the early 1960s, planning for NATO military forces revolved around two major issues. One of these, the manipulation of NATO nuclear power—primarily American, but also that of Britain, and later France—so that the nonnuclear Europeans would feel protected while the number of "fingers on the trigger" was kept minimal, is not the subject here. No way was ever found to solve the logical contradiction between independent and interdependent nuclear control, and by the late 1960s the issue had faded out completely.

The second NATO planning issue concerned the military forces on the European continent. As the 1960s progressed, it became clear that, for whatever reason, NATO forces could not be expected to defeat a determined Soviet and Warsaw Pact attack without using nuclear weapons. Why this was and what could be done about it was the substantive subject matter of much of the planning, but there was little doubt at any given time that a full nonnuclear defense was lacking. At the same time as it became clear that nonnuclear defense against determined massive Soviet attack was impossible, however, it also became clear that such a Soviet attack, the chief military reason for the existence of NATO, was very unlikely. And simultaneously, the other military function of NATO, keeping control of German forces, also became much less important as German political and military responsibility became much more firmly fixed in the minds of the other members of the alliance.

Given all this, and adding to it the budgetary pressures in all NATO countries to spend on national objectives other than defense, military planning diverged sharply from reality and exhibited some drawbacks that, though typical perhaps of much military planning and operations, were not obvious in the strategic cases discussed above.

Through the 1960s, NATO military planning and the analysis behind that planning continued to revolve around the building and deploying of ground and air forces against the nearly nonexistent massive Soviet threat, in contrast to military-political planning and analysis that might have examined the political basis of the alliance and made recommendations for reconstructing both the political and military force posture so as to fulfill the aims of NATO and its members. Since policy-making itself was in fact political (NATO force policies were determined almost entirely by the political imperatives brought into the alliance by its members), the military planning itself became increasingly divorced from the political realities and ended up having little to do with any real policy at all. This in itself may have been all right. If all parties had treated the meager nonnuclear capability to meet the highly improbable threat as a set of conventions by which the real aims of NATO could be furthered (for example, deterrence of lesser Communist aggression while promoting political stability) without mentioning embarrassing political realities (a "social myth"), nothing would have been wasted but money. But by the mid-1960s, the myth began to diverge so much from reality that it was losing its utility.

The military debate, even as late as 1968, might be typified by the following exchange between Alain Enthoven, U.S. Assistant Secretary of Defense for Systems Analysis, and the House of Representatives Committee on Armed Services Special Subcommittee on National Defense Posture. Enthoven had presented to NATO a comparative evaluation of NATO and Warsaw Pact nonnuclear forces that may be fairly characterized by the following quotes:

> The purpose today is to discuss our reasons for believing that a satisfactory nonnuclear capability is feasible at about current planned budgets, provided plans are made and carried out to supply, protect and use NATO's existing forces effectively. . . .
>
> Military assessments have continually concluded that NATO would be hopelessly outnumbered almost immediately in any sizeable conventional war. . . .
>
> These assessments are a logical result of the normally sound military principle of never underestimating the threat. However, when political conditions make it impossible to supply the forces necessary to meet the threat when so conservatively defined, the result can be dangerous. Instead of supporting fully adequate forces, which is viewed as politically and economically impossible, many people conclude that NATO's military forces are so hopelessly inadequate as to be nearly irrelevant. . . .
>
> Although it is difficult or even impossible to predict the outcome of future wars, it is possible to develop useful indicators of relative capability.
>
> If these indicators are used to compare the forces, it becomes apparent that certain weaknesses in the structure and support of the forces are very important, and can be corrected at relatively small cost.[5]

But the subcommittee's view of Enthoven's analysis was quite negative, negative not because of any possible irrelevance to the political needs of the alliance but negative on Enthoven's own military grounds:

> U.S. NATO representatives were toiling in February of 1968 again seeking to make the other member nations understand that

unless NATO were significantly strengthened, it would no longer be an effective force, either militarily or politically.

It was at this point that Dr. Enthoven appeared on the scene with his "Methodology for Evaluating Conventional Forces." The effect of this on the best laid plans of our top U.S. NATO military advisers will not be known for some time to come, but it could hardly be accurate to describe it as helpful. During hearings held by the subcommittee it was described as having had an extremely harmful effect. Dr. Enthoven began his presentation by telling the NATO group that there is no reason for them to increase their currently planned military budgets or the size of their existing forces; that present NATO forces are at least equal to Warsaw Pact forces. If he is right, our best military advisers are wrong; but on the basis of sworn testimony and documentary evidence which the subcommittee has assembled, the subcommittee finds adequate reason to question the validity of Dr. Enthoven's position. . . .

If Dr. Enthoven's analysis, as employed in this presentation, represents the state of the art of systems analysis, the subcommittee cannot accept its employment for strategic planning. Nor does it provide a basis for consultation with the alliance members on political and military matters. We believe that the presentation suffers from serious oversimplification of some facts and failure to consider others. Systems analysis does have a value and it can provide methods for analyzing and defining a given problem, but we think it a very poor vehicle for arriving at absolute solutions. Even if all the data were correct, and the comparisons and criteria reliable, the presentation appears to have as its principal thrust the achievement of parity between NATO and the Warsaw Pact. We think that the goal should be superiority, not parity. This methodology for evaluating conventional forces by employing a systems analysis technique produces little in the way of instruction and much to undermine our announced U.S. objectives. . . .

The subcommittee is now as convinced as ever that there remains a substantial place for military experience, judgment, and professional expertise in military decision-making and in military consultations with our allies.[6]

In fact, the debate between Enthoven and his congressional opponents was unreal on both sides. The committee spoke in terms of the politically impossible objective of increasing NATO forces. Enthoven contended that those forces could be improved at little or no extra cost but had nothing to say about how, in fact, the desired improvements (desired, at least, by civilian planners like Enthoven) might be put through the military structure of the American armed forces. This military structure, in other NATO countries as well as the United States, meant that the desirable was then unachievable, and no planner or analyst had yet come to grips with how it might be made achievable. During late 1969, at least one West Point trained military analyst, Steven Canby, laid the problem out succinctly:

There seems to be unanimous agreement among military officers that U.S. Forces in Europe have been so reduced since 1965 that further cutbacks can only be made by seriously downgrading assigned missions. Most also believe that the earlier OSD imposed reductions which focused on the logistical tail have so unbalanced the Army's force posture that further cuts must largely come from the combat units in order to restore the desired balance. After reviewing the Army's wartime deployment plans and peacetime operating modes, I believe this assertion is correct. However, I also believe that resources are being misused, and that major increases in combat capability or conversely troop reductions are possible.

The key question is how to induce or pressure the military into more efficient practices. It might seem that the military ought to know best how to make any change, and that threatened reductions which may impair the mission ought to produce more efficiency. However, the military invariably recommend reduced unit strengths, proportional withdrawals of a wide spectrum of units, and disproportionate cuts in end output combat units—all solutions bypassing the question of efficiency. One basic reason why such pressures/constraints upon specific theaters do not induce more efficient behavior is that their commanders do not have the entrepreneurial authority to deviate from standard practices in tactics, organization, purchasing, and myriad other procedures determined by the Army Staff, Army Materiel Command, and Combat Developments Command. Yet if efficiency is to be induced, it is precisely these practices which must be analyzed and changed. Pressure upon the theater commanders can at best have only an indirect and marginal impact upon these policies which "drive" the Army's *modus operandi*.[7]

But laying it out this way was only the beginning of the kind of planning that might improve the force effectiveness to the Enthoven point, and this was in 1969 after at least a decade of such debates.

In any case, the problem was not only in the military structure and not really mainly with military effectiveness of forces, not so long as the Soviet threat against which these forces were supposed to be effective did not much exist anyhow. In the final analysis NATO was a political not a military alliance, and even force planning to be realistic would have had to take into account in a major way the political factors. The real problem of NATO planning was described during 1966 by Andrew Marshall:

What is of primary importance is the fact that the ultimate decisions as to budgetary allocations among military services, missions, weapons procurement programs, etc. are made by the several countries. This means that there are at least 12 separate decision centers that in aggregate determine each year by their decisions the gradual evolution of the military forces of the European NATO Allies. Moreover, in the case of each of these countries, there are many separate forces which bear upon the relevant decisions. The separate military services of each country, national munitions industries, and many other government ministries, in addition to the ministries of defense, are interested parties. In any case, the various bureaucratic elements and political groups within a given country have an impact upon the decisions of its government as to procurement of weapons, the supply of military manpower, its length of service, etc., that ultimately determine the effectiveness of the forces that country provides to NATO. Too often the bureaucratic, economic, and social factors that so strongly influence individual country's behavior are lumped loosely under the rubric "political" without further differentiation or analysis. Some of the factors are perhaps largely political in the sense that they reflect either specific internal political issues or are related to the external political ambitions of particular nations. But a great number of them are political in only a secondary way and are reflections of the bureaucratic and economic interest of groups within a country and/or its government.[8]

In fact, in 1965, Norman Jones and I had tried to begin in a preliminary way a kind of planning analysis that would have been required to make NATO's military force posture meaningful for the political objectives of the organization:

To preserve the Alliance, ... a posture should try to satisfy (or at least not violate) the felt needs of the members, and we thus can arrive at a set of political criteria, based on these needs, which a posture should strive to meet. That a limited-war posture give some satisfaction to these needs seems a necessary condition for NATO's continued existence; although even if they were fully satisfied, the Alliance could still falter over some other issue such as nuclear control. The criteria are not absolute, of course (particularly since some of them are conflicting), but they are important:

1. Because the Federal Republic of Germany is under the gun, its expectation of Soviet aggression is likely to remain high, no matter what our beliefs. Thus the limited-war posture should not reduce the visible token of the U.S. (and other) commitment to the defense of West Germany more than is tolerable to the West Germans. In current practice this means a commitment not substantially less than the present five or six American divisions.

2. The posture should not symbolize the permanent division of Germany, either through unmistakable physical signs or through a degree of *detente* which signifies "permanent" stability along present boundaries.

3. A political criterion bound to be imposed by the United States is that the posture should include tight centralized control of all nuclear weapons without preauthorized use.

4. The posture should not demand substantially larger contributions in either money or manpower from NATO members, since it seems abundantly clear that these will not be forthcoming, and the demand itself is divisive.

5. The posture should be able to contain any French attempts to disrupt the alliance or set it up on a new "Europe-only" basis which might not suffice either to deter the Russians or satisfy the Germans.

6. The posture should pay enough attention to NATO's flanks both to satisfy the security needs felt by the flank countries, and to satisfy Germany that the Central Front will remain secure during a flank crisis.

7. The posture should be able to adapt to even lower budgets without collapsing.

8. The posture should have some sort of hedge or gap-filler to prevent the Russians, or a threatened ally, or (perhaps most important) SACEUR [Supreme Allied Commander, Europe], from feeling that there are some aggressions that can be carried out with impunity.

Since political imperatives like those listed will not suffice to obtain popular and governmental support for a posture, however, some military rationale is still needed, as a binding ideological force for the chosen posture. That is, a posture based on an explicit statement that its major purpose is to calm unwarranted German fears is not likely to hold Britain in the Alliance, nor will it encourage Germany, or for that matter the United States. Because of this, some ostensible (and perhaps real) military purpose is needed for the limited-war posture—some frame of reference in which a plausible military explanation can be made.

The threat of an all-out Soviet invasion of Western Europe seems to have outlived its usefulness as a rationale, primarily because few governments or people still believe it to be realistic. Defending against this threat, however, has held NATO's joint institutions together until now, and it may be that no other rationale will substitute. If this is true, then it may be necessary to hold to the old rationale even though it may collapse and bring the Alliance down with it.

It may be possible, however, to substitute another rationale for the all-out attack. One possible situation around which such a rationale for limited-war posture can be built, therefore, is a smaller action—a Soviet grab at Berlin or its lifelines, or at some other part of Germany. Together with this sort of overt military action goes its shadow, the "crisis," which can be defined as an affair in which political or nonshooting military moves are made which increase the risk of open military hostilities. The crisis may provide the best foundation on which to built a rationale.[9]

The point is not that we were right in 1965. The reader familiar with NATO will recognize points at which with hindsight we can be seen to have been wrong, and some of the 1965 readers had the foresight to see it then. The real point, however, is that this kind of planning for military force posture seemed then and seems now to be called for and has very seldom if ever been carried out systematically.

Military Policy in "Third Areas": Vietnam

If the failure of American military planning for NATO was essentially a failure to grasp the real point about the motivations of nations we knew well, the failure in Vietnam was a much more general one. In Vietnam, as in other "third areas," it was and is difficult to figure out what the point is at all. American motivations and constraints have been unclear, and our understanding of the other parties at interest has been practically nonexistent.

As suggested above, American military policy has been able to deal well, if wastefully, with the problem of strategic war and deterrence, for which a simplified model based on rationality has sufficed. Once we moved away from situations where this model was applicable, however, the whole world began to become very soft and fuzzy. A year after the Cuban missile crisis of 1962, I wrote:

This leaning toward the tangibility of power in its military forms is . . . illustrated by the . . . attitude toward Cuba before, during, and after the 1962 crisis over the Soviet missiles. Before the presentation of clear evidence that Soviet "offensive weapons" were being sited on the island, [there was] no clear view about what to do about either Castro or the Soviet buildup of "defensive" weapons in Cuba; indeed, there was some tendency to sweep the problem under the rug and to feel that the most important thing was not to allow Cuba to distract us from the real problem in Berlin. . . . With the coming of the knowledge of the presence of the Soviet ballistic missiles in Cuba, however, there also came a feeling of intellectual relief. . . . This was a truly military question, and a rather narrowly strategic one at that. Questions of this nature had been studied, the available set of alternatives was well understood, and the proper one could be selected. And finally, with our seeming success in getting rid of the missiles, the question of Cuba and Castro returned . . . to the category of an imprecise one, in which it was very difficult to find the proper mixture of military and other forms of power.[10]

At the same time, in discussing the Vietnam problem which was then relatively new in 1962, I analyzed the viewpoints of the moderate left, the middle, and the moderate right. In reviewing now what was said then by those who commented on Vietnam, it is striking that nobody had an answer that looks in retrospect as if it would have worked. The middle wanted the continued application of military power in a way that by 1965 led to the verge of defeat. The right wanted the kind of escalation that since 1965 has turned defeat into disaster. And the moderate left was looking for a middle of the road democratic government of the sort that never has been available in Vietnam.

All this suggests one type of failure of the planning of military policy in Vietnam. This sort of planning, like almost all other planning, must necessarily be incremental, one small step at a time, in order to be realistic. Planning realism always leads to incrementalism, and indeed, even the recommendations in the final chapters of this book for new sorts of planning are incremental; yet in some situations, incrementalism simply does not suffice. In retrospect, it looks as if the best policy for Vietnam during 1963 would have been to get out, lock, stock, and barrel; yet this seemed completely unrealistic at the time. In retrospect, perhaps we could have gotten out. If Kennedy had lived, perhaps he would have; maybe Johnson could have taken advantage of the transition honeymoon to do so. And certainly many planners and analysts now retrospectively favor having gotten out during 1963. But, back then, getting out was the viewpoint of a few radicals who were not taken seriously by the sober incrementalists.

In any case, Vietnam has been such a complete fiasco that it provides a rather complete catalog of all the possible flaws in military planning (by both civilians and military men) and all the limits of planning in a complicated situation. If the first and most significant planning failure was the failure of incrementalism, the second was the failure to understand politics well enough to plan in a political context. That we failed to understand Vietnamese politics is obvious. As such, this failure might lead only to the implication that we ought not plan complicated strategies for exotic lands with which we have a low degree of empathy. In fact, however, and far more important, the planners of American military policy (the civilian planners as much or more than the military) also failed to include American politics in their calculations, and this has much wider implications for planning. As indicated in the evidence previously adduced, planning, whether domestic or military, typically has failed to include political factors; Vietnam is one more case in point.

It seems obvious, looking backward from the 1970s at the

withdrawal of Lyndon Johnson from the 1968 presidential campaign and the troubles of President Nixon from 1969 onward, that American politics has had everything to do with the planning of military policy for Vietnam. Yet, in the early-1960s discussions of "limited war," domestic politics was considered only a minor constraining factor. In one of the most perceptive of the analyses of this time period, published in 1963, Morton Halperin devoted only two pages of a 131-page book on limited war to domestic politics.[11] The two pages happened to be quite prescient; Halperin said, for example, "it is possible that the Administration will view a decision to intervene with combat forces in a local war as entailing great domestic political costs. . . . What will prove most unpopular domestically will be the continuation of fighting without a clear-cut decision." But it was still only two pages. And in any case, the actual planners of the Vietnam war nearly ignored the domestic political reactions that later came to control the war.

If the first two failures—the failure of incrementalism and the failure to consider politics—were the responsibility of civilian planners at high levels as well as low, the third was a failure more within the realm of the military men. This was the failure of military doctrine for a conventional, that is, nonnuclear, ground war to adapt to a counterinsurgency effort in a tropical country. It is a cliché that the Army always fights the last war. In spite of President Kennedy's efforts to create a doctrine and the forces for counterinsurgency (the Green Berets), all the American military services fought in Vietnam the kind of war they had fought (or would have liked to have fought) in Korea. The Army and Marine Corps worked hard to adapt relatively large-unit warfare to the pursuit of an elusive enemy in the jungle, and their labor gave birth to the helicopter. (It might be argued that rather than refighting the Korean War, the Army tried to refight the nineteenth-century wars against the Plains Indians.) The Air Force bombed, adapting its weapons but not its style of warfare to the new situation. The Navy stood offshore and bombarded (and it, too, refought an earlier war, with the "riverine" fleet in the Mekong Delta resembling in some respects the Mississippi Delta fleet of the Civil War). Not all this was wrong, given the underlying doctrine of meeting an enemy and shooting him up as the basic core of received military doctrine. But the doctrinal core itself was seldom questioned and was generally inapplicable.

This leads to the fourth failure of planning, one that illustrates the intricate interplay between civilian and soldier. It is not that nobody knew better than to apply the inapplicable doctrine. But that the suggestions of those who did know better fell unheeded is as much the failure of planning to be effective as was the bad planning that was carried into execution. There are those who contend, for example, that the Marine Corps did in fact develop an effective doctrine of counterinsurgency warfare, one based more on static policing of hamlets than on mobile search and destroy. But the doctrine never took hold and the Marines themselves ended up outdoing the Army in Army-style large-unit warfare in the northern part of South Vietnam. Perhaps there were other important and viable suggestions for counterinsurgency. Their content is not important here, however; what is important is to ask why even that good planning that was available helped little.

There are at least two reasons. One is related to the previously mentioned failure of military doctrine. It was the failure of the good planners—military officers as well as civilians—to cope with the military decision-making machine that had to implement the plans. Canby's statement, quoted above, on the difficulties of inducing change with regard to NATO in the military machine applies at least as sharply to Vietnam. The professional officer corps is and always has been highly inbred. It has known what is right, has maintained this right stubbornly, and has promoted those officers who agreed to the truth. If the right turns out to be wrong, or the true to be false, it is virtually impossible either to convince the machine or to force it to change its ways against its will. Forcing major changes in doctrine through the military machine has typically been the work of decades, as in the case of air power both on land and at sea. And the air doctrine changes, it must be noted, were forced through by military men. The military has guarded its prerogative to write the operational plans and to push the definitional border of "operational" far into the realms of doctrine and force planning. In the limit, this would leave to civilians only the decision as to total force size and the go-no-go decision whether to go to war using the military men's plans.

Nor is the American military machine atypical; if anything, it is more flexible than most. Indeed, this is not necessarily a criticism of the military machine; it is entirely possible that this is the only way that an operation so dependent on discipline can run at all; certainly the universality of the evidence indicates this. But it is a major constraint on military planning. Military men do not—indeed, on the basis of their doctrine, cannot—execute the "good" plans of civilians. And the incentive system within the military structure does not bring up many good planners within the services themselves.

Thus, as things stand now, the main lesson for civilian planners of grand strategy is that even the best effort to point out what should be done becomes rather irrelevant if it cannot or will not be done by the military machine charged with its implementation. And, indeed, the difficulties with implementation by the military are perhaps a magnification of the difficulties in carrying a civilian program through the permanent bureaucracy; the problems are quite similar. Increasingly, implementation is being recognized as the basic problem of both civil and military planning. But how to go about changing this is unknown and unexplored.

In addition to the failure to penetrate the military machine, the good planners of Vietnam failed for a more generalized reason: The "signal to noise ratio" was just too low. As Roberta Wohlstetter has pointed out, the failure of intelligence at Pearl Harbor was not so much a failure to detect what the Japanese were doing. We detected what they were doing, we also detected many things that we thought they were doing that they were not doing, and we did not know which to take seriously.[12] Similarly, Vietnam was such a big affair and so many planners and advisers were saying so many different things that it was tough or impossible to distinguish between the good data and the bad, or the good planning and the bad. And this constraint on any effort to improve planning by doing more planning seems generalizable beyond the military case. Good planning does not drive out the bad, nor is the reverse true. They coexist, and nobody can tell which is which.

The same general civilian intellectual community that provided (or may have provided, or seemed to provide) good planning advice that was not utilized in Vietnam did, however, provide one other piece of carefully thought out doctrine that was used. It was used, and it formed the basis for converting failure into disaster. What was provided here was the rational underpinning for the bombing of North Vietnam and the continuing escalation of the war, which led to the Vietnam war's taking its place as the unsolvable issue splitting American society. It is not that nonservice military planners either directly suggested the escalation strategy to President Johnson or orchestrated it; I have no knowledge of the inside-government processes that went on. Certainly the normal desire of the Air Force to drop bombs had a lot to do with it, and it seems likely that not only the design, but the direct recommendation for the escalation stemmed from the military.

Nonetheless, nonmilitary thinking validated a military desire that might otherwise have been discounted because of its source. The writings of the civilian analysts of the early and mid-1960s created the atmosphere that made escalation seem much more firmly founded in logical rationality than would otherwise have been the case. Without these writings, the military desire for escalation might have been dismissed by top civilian decision-makers. The military is traditionally impatient with "artificial" bounds, and MacArthur was fired when he tried too hard to transcend them. But to some of the major civilian advisers, escalation looked like a perfectly reasonable step in 1964–1965.

What seems to have occurred is that the development of strategic planning doctrine during the late 1950s and early 1960s, discussed above, led in turn to refinements of the doctrine of the use of escalation and threats of escalation as a political-military device. This doctrine, in turn, made escalation in Vietnam seem a reasonable thing to do with a substantial chance of success. Key to the development of the doctrine was Thomas

Schelling, who, in two influential books of the early and mid-1960s, first developed a theory of the use of strategic threats and then put the theory into various policy contexts.[13] It is not that Schelling directed or advised the Vietnam escalation strategy. A detailed reading indicates that he was quite careful about hedging any explicit or implicit recommendations. But he was inclined to look at the strategy as at least an attempt to apply the sort of thing he was talking about:

> The bombing of North Vietnam . . . was not an all-out interdiction campaign, exclusively designed to cut supplies to the Vietcong; had it been that, there would have been little reason not to do the bombing on a larger scale at the outset. The bombing had an evident measure of coercive intent behind it: it was evidently designed, at least partly, to inflict plain loss of value on the adversary until he began to behave. The bombing was widely discussed, and sometimes explained by the Administration, as a means of putting pressure on the government of North Vietnam; and when extension to industrial establishments was discussed, it was not mainly in terms of slowing down the enemy's war effort but of raising the cost of not coming to terms. The occasional hints and actual instances of conditional cessation of the bombing in North Vietnam, in contrast to that in the south, were to be sought in North Vietnamese willingness to comply, to accommodate, to withdraw, or to negotiate (as well as in setting a pattern, and possibly a warning, for the contingency of Communist Chinese participation).[14]

Schelling has claimed that he had severe doubts about the strategy and the claim seems valid in the light of his written work. Nonetheless, Schelling's ideas were a very important part of the intellectual atmosphere surrounding political-military decision-making of the 1960s. The conditions he placed on the applicability of the ideas were subtle, and it seems highly possible that these ideas came through to key planners without a full understanding of the conditions and qualifications. Subtle ideas are frequently heard unsubtly, which is one more limitation on detailed planning.

The final failure of planning in Vietnam was the failure to realize that perhaps there was no solution. In a way this says the same thing as the statement of the first failure, the failure of planning to reach beyond incrementalism. The spirit behind the failure to realize the possibility of no answer, however, is somewhat different. Incrementalism is largely a matter of style; it could conceivably be changed within the context of planning; belief in the possibility of a solution is inherent in planning. If there is no way out, why try?

Perhaps no solution was available, and failure to realize this was the ultimate failure. Nonetheless, it is still very tempting to say that there was a solution, that we did it wrong but could have done it right. The catalog of failures listed above suggests that this is not the case, however; that there was no Vietnam solution (or at least no incremental solution) possibly accessible to good planning. Going through some of the failures discussed:

1. We could have avoided the disaster of escalation by substituting better thought-out planning for poorer planning. Had we avoided escalation, we might well have avoided the degree of national and international debacle that followed. But holding constant all the other failures, avoiding escalation probably would have meant substituting quick, small defeat for slow, large disaster, or so it appeared during 1965.

2. More central was the failure to bring into the planning process an understanding of Vietnamese politics. Such an understanding seems crucial to any possibility of actually having won the Vietnam war, defining winning modestly enough as the removal of the American presence from Vietnam, leaving behind a governmental structure with some reasonable chance of remaining non-Communist. But it is doubtful that it is possible to plan our way through politics this way, even if we understand them. Certainly there are no easily applicable rules for understanding and applying the politics of underdeveloped countries to the art of counterinsurgency. And we are thus faced once again with the dilemma of rules interpreted according to highly imperfect human discretion.

3. Even if we suspend the political criteria and consider the war a purely military matter, the failure to cope with the military machine as it is—and as it perhaps necessarily is—would have precluded a military victory. Yet, again it seems very difficult to conceive of the kind of good planning that might have

caused the military machine to achieve the possible military solution.

This, then, is the real answer. Even if good planning were possible in this intensely complex situation, its implementation would not be possible, and this fact alone denies the definition of goodness for planning. Vietnam has been so intricate a fiasco that it has had and will have many lessons for every aspect of science, social science, and philosophy. Its chief lesson for planning is as an illustration that the planners cannot lay out a course from here to there through any such jungle of complexity.

Notes

1. Stephane Groueff, *Manhattan Project* (New York: Bantam Books, 1967), p. 11.
2. Burton H. Klein, *Germany's Economic Preparations for War* (Cambridge: Harvard University Press, 1959), p. 231.
3. Data from *Jane's Fighting Ships, 1968–1969* (London: Sampson, Low, Marston & Co., Ltd., 1968), p. 411.
4. Albert Wohlstetter, "The Delicate Balance of Terror," *Foreign Affairs,* 37, no. 2 (January 1959): 212–222. Copyright 1959 by the Council on Foreign Relations, Inc., New York.
5. U.S. Congress, Committee on Armed Services, Special Subcommittee on National Defense Posture, "Review of a Systems Analysis Evaluation of NATO vs. Warsaw Pact Conventional Forces" (Washington: Government Printing Office, 1967), pp. 8–15.
6. *Ibid.,* pp. 2–7.
7. Steven L. Canby, unpublished paper, September 26, 1969, p. 2.
8. A. W. Marshall, *Determinants of NATO Force Posture,* Rand Corporation Paper P–3280, January 1966, p. 4.
9. N. H. Jones, Jr., and R. A. Levine, unpublished paper, 1965, pp. vi–viii.
10. Robert A. Levine, *The Arms Debate* (Cambridge: Harvard University Press, 1963), pp. 201–202.
11. Morton H. Halperin, *Limited War for the Nuclear Age* (New York: Wiley, 1963), pp. 24–25.
12. Roberta Wohlstetter, *Pearl Harbor: Warning and Decision* (Stanford: Stanford University Press, 1962).
13. Thomas Schelling, *Strategy of Conflict* (Cambridge: Harvard University Press, 1960); *Arms and Influence* (New Haven: Yale University Press, 1966).
14. Schelling, *Arms and Influence,* p. 17.

5

Entremet

INDUCTIVE REASONING can prove nothing, in any final sense. The evidence of the last two chapters makes a strong case that systems depending on a high degree of administration, with implementation by human beings following complex plans or sets of rules, tend to fail. Only under the special conditions and criteria of wartime or planning for war have they met the expectations of the system designers. And the conditions for the presumed success of strategic planning and the partial success of wartime production controls were very special indeed. Other administered systems, including other military ones, have failed. Yet, it is always possible to argue that "If we had just done it better, it would have worked."

My contention, finally unprovable, but seemingly borne out by the evidence, is that it would not have worked, not if it was this sort of administered system. The setting forth of plans and rules for their implementation does not ordinarily lead toward the objectives for which these plans and rules were initially written.

Sometimes the problem is with self-interest: individual self-interest getting around the rules as in the case of NRA; individual interest staying within the rules and ending up perverting the purposes as in Urban Renewal. Nor need the self-interest be individual only. NATO planners failed to build the intended kind of force posture in Western Europe because of the obdurate insistence of national politicians in the NATO countries on following national objectives, which had largely been ignored by the planners.

Sometimes the problem is with conflicting plans, rules, and doctrines, as in the intersection of civilian and military planning in Vietnam. Sometimes the plans are simply not rich enough in considering assumptions and alternatives: the failure of Vietnam planners to bring either Vietnam or American politics into their plans; their failure to take seriously nonincremental alternatives.

Perhaps the most general cause of failure, however, is inherent in administered systems. It is the inability of the human mind to devise plans and rules that it can adequately follow. This is best illustrated by the more routinely bureaucratic operating systems that have been discussed. Rules have failed to operate satisfactorily in the case of the property tax, the military draft, the welfare system, and the federal-state-local education and manpower systems. In each of these, decision-makers have laid out an explicit or implicit model of the way things should work, and they have laid out rules for things to happen that way. For the property tax, assessors should be able to follow clear rules for establishing value, and these rules should be such that taxes are in reasonable proportion to the wealth being taxed. In the case of the draft, the rules are supposed to lead to equity in the liability to military service and combat. For welfare, the rules are supposed to clearly distinguish between the eligible and the ineligible and to determine for each eligible the amount of support needed. For education, the rules attached to federal fund distribution are supposed to direct the monies to those districts and students most in need and those projects most likely to succeed, and similarly for the federal-state-local manpower system.

And, as seems quite obvious, in none of these systems does following the rules lead to the desired objectives. On remarkably few occasions are the rules broken. It is just that following them does not lead anywhere near the hoped-for goal. The problem here is not self-interest getting around the rules or preventing their application; it is that honest attempts at expressing the public interest through rules and their applications turn out to be perverse. And to compound all this, the ordinary administrative ethos is that if the rules do not work, as they obviously do not, the solution lies in adding more rules and interpretations of the rules until vast volumes of administrative law are created and the system is no better off than it was initially. Similarly, when bureaucratic organizations do not work well, as mostly they do not, the solution is generally to add coordinators, expediters, new layers of administrators, and so forth. This is the stuff that Parkinson's and other laws are made of. It has at least reached the point where it is possible to get a good laugh.

The basis of the problem seems to be the variability of human beings and the limitations of the human mind in trying to follow precise systems as intended. What it seems to come to is that if precise, unambiguous rules for public policy governing social systems were possible, then in this day and age such rules could be programmed for a computer (as indeed, have many of the rules for distribution of Social Security payments and for administration of at least the simple version of the individual income tax). And, given the relative economics of computers and intellectual labor, they probably ought to be so programmed. But computer logic is unforgiving and tolerates no ambiguities. Rules as written for social systems are ambiguous, cannot be used by a computer, and must perforce be interpreted by the administrative discretion of people. And the remaining administrative discretion, definitionally not completely guided by its own rules, depends on a complex human calculus.

The human decision-making calculus is by no means motivated by self-interest alone. It is made up of different sorts of elements: self-interest, personal altruism, institutional interest, and honest desire to achieve public objectives. However, self-interest assumes a particular importance because none of this human calculus is well understood except for self-interest. And even within the realm of self-interest, the only case of such interest that has been studied in its logical implications as well as its psychological sources is economic self-interest, the economic man.

This, as much as anything, is the real attraction of the market system as a device for carrying out public policy. The market system in its private or public manifestations is attractive because of the smoothness of its operation and its economically defined efficiency in providing a basket of goods that bears some relation to consumer desires. But its specific attractiveness for utilization in public policy lies in the fact that we think we understand economic man and in understanding we can vary his direction by varying his incentives. We thus have a mechanism for policy expression that is both operable in a smooth fashion and apparently guidable toward public objectives. Perhaps systems operating on the basis of political self-interest, such as the bargaining systems discussed above, can be operated as smoothly and guided as neatly, but at this point in time we do not understand political self-interest as well as economic self-interest and are therefore likely to be more clumsy with the political systems. And insofar as bureaucratic systems are concerned, we understand so little about bureaucratic self-interest, both in itself and in relation to the other elements of bureaucratic motivation—public interest and altruism—that we can operate bureaucratic systems almost not at all.

So what we come to on the basis of the evidence presented so far, is that rules do not work, planning in the ordinary sense of laying out rules to move from here to there does not work, and implementation by following rules does not work. Rather, we are forced willy-nilly to look for broad-brush programs, self-applied and incentive-guided, as exemplified by the market systems, the business cycle control systems, and the income tax systems discussed above. Such self-applied systems are decentralized by definition; they are operated through the ultimate decentralization mechanism of every man for himself. But the logic does not work the other way; self-applied incentive systems are necessarily decentralized, but decentralized systems are not necessarily self-applied or incentive guided. And when they are not, as in the cases of the property tax and the draft, they work no better than centralized systems.

All this leads then to the attempts to apply market types of systems to public policy. And yet this application is not perfect and leads to substantial doubts. It leads to doubts primarily because the market is not even-handed in its results. Inherent in the market system—in any self-interest system—is the fact that the fruits of the system go to the strong. This is the distribution problem: the problem of income distribution and the problem of power distribution. Strength leads to greater strength, and the result is not acceptable under modern democratic ethics. To be sure political bargaining can compensate to some extent for the distributional inequities of economic markets. The economically strong are not necessarily identical to the politically strong, though there is certainly a very frequent correspondence, and at least there is some chance for political power to countervail economic power. But on grounds of distribution if no other grounds, self-interest systems leave much to be desired.

In terms of effectiveness in achieving efficient and equitable results, the system of balancing out economic markets and political marketplaces scarcely seems sufficient; but given the current state of bureaucratic administration, it is pretty much what we have to depend on for results. Yet, since the economic market and political bargaining modes suggested above simply fail to cover all bases of public policy operations, we must begin learning to deal with bureaucracies as well. Public bureaucracy exists, and it is not going to go away. Some 12 million Americans, 18 percent of the total labor force, are public employees at all levels of government. This proportion is not likely to decrease substantially; nor can it disappear. Even after much heavier weight than at present is put on the economic and political marketplaces, bureaucracies must at a minimum administer the governmental portions of these other programs; a bureaucracy administers the Federal Reserve System as it affects cyclical policy; a bureaucracy administers the Community Action Program as it changes bargaining forces within urban areas. A huge bureaucracy operates the military service and must continue to do so; the idea of turning all force over to the private market has no appeal. But most of all, because governmental bureaucracy exists in such large size, it has an immense potential for good as well as for evil if we could learn to deal with it.

And dealing with bureaucracy is not a lost cause. If we can treat bureaucracy as it actually is, if we can understand bureaucratic incentives as well as we understand some private economic ones, the bureaucratic mode too can be utilized for public policy. This understanding is just beginning; it is to understanding bureaucracy that this study next turns.

6 Working with Bureaucracy

BUREAUCRACY EXISTS, and in any modern society bureaucratic government will continue to exist. In many areas it will simply be impossible to substitute private instrumentalities for governmental ones. Yet, bureaucracy works poorly in achieving the objectives of the programs it is supposed to administer. This is the paradox. It is a paradox for planners who design public programs that must be administered by bureaucracies. It is a paradox that has been increasingly analyzed by students of public administration.

During recent years, bureaucracy has been studied from bottom to top: from the detailed analyses of intraorganizational relations in bureaucracy by March and Simon [1] and Downs [2] to Neustadt's book of precepts for Presidents.[3] The standpoint of this chapter and this book is between these extremes, though closer to Neustadt. The question of what to do about bureaucracy is approached from the point of view of the policy-level government official who is responsible for trying to get results from a program costing many hundreds of millions or even billions of dollars. The viewpoint is not that of the President, who has his own unique problems, but perhaps that of a Cabinet member, the head of a major government agency, top staff planners and advisers to such officials, and the legislators who create the programs.

Such officials must design and set up operating systems in ways in which they might conceivably work for the policy objectives of programs. It is clear that to set up such a system with any hope of its working, one must understand operations in a bureaucracy: how things will work through to field-level government employees and contractors and to clients. But understanding these operations is different from carrying them out; the top officials cannot supervise operations in detail, nor can they supervise the supervisors except those of the highest stratum. Perceptive studies such as those of March and Simon and of Downs, as well as Michel Crozier's analysis of French bureaucracies,[4] are prescriptive, to the extent that they are prescriptive at all, for those who want to run a particular organizational unit. For top decision-makers, however, they are cautionary and constraining but provide no direct information as to what to do to make an overall policy work. From this level the bureaucracy is a set of black boxes. It may be possible to change the production run of boxes (how to change the bureaucracy is one subject of this chapter), but it makes little sense for the operator of a system with hundreds of black boxes to open them and tinker with them one by one.

A major reason for the lack of direct applicability of detailed studies of bureaucracy and for the difficulty in getting a policy executed as designed in a bureaucracy, then, is the diffusion of decision-making through large numbers of operating units. Such diffusion is the reason the market system does work; paradoxically, it is why bureaucracy does not.

In the federal bureaucracy, the President may say, "Do this"; the Cabinet members, hearing him slightly imperfectly, through their own ears and interests, will instruct their subordinates slightly differently, and so on down the line, with the line necessarily being a long one in a large complex operation. Statistically, the likelihood of everything being done as intended by the policy designers is close to zero. And the crucial point is that a bureaucratic operation, unlike the market, is one in which most of the black boxes are connected in series so that any error, misinterpretation, or deviation will be multiplied and magnified throughout the system. Bureaucratic chains are very sensitive to their weakest links.

Exceptions to this seem to occur only when the top leader takes direct charge of the tiniest details of operation. In Graham Allison's study of the 1965 Cuban missile crisis [5] as interpreted alternatively as a problem in rational decision-making, a problem in organizational activity, and a problem in interorganizational bureaucratic conflict, he points out that President Kennedy, in order to have his orders carried out on the timing of the Cuban blockade, the location of the line not to be crossed, and the style of approach to Soviet vessels, had to give these orders in the detail ordinarily associated with the commands of a commodore commanding a destroyer flotilla. And Secretary McNamara was his executive officer, giving direct commands on ship maneuvers to Chief of Naval Operations Admiral Anderson. Even so, Allison suggests that Navy efforts to interpret the orders according to the manual of Navy regulations led to the blockade being located further from Cuba than the President wanted. All this was a matter of high policy because the President wanted to give Khrushchev every bit of time available to consider giving in; it was a matter of controversy because the Naval Command, hearing the orders, still interpreted them according to received doctrine. And the point is that this time it worked; if it did not work precisely as the President wanted, the outcome turned out not to be sensitive to Navy misinterpretation. It worked, but it worked because the President of the United States and the Secretary of Defense acted at a level of detail possible only in situations of the greatest gravity. A somewhat parallel domestic example is the 1962 rollback of steel price increases, when President Kennedy and his brother, the Attorney General, operated in detail on the presidents of the major companies. Both in domestic and international affairs, these instances must be rare and the Presidential power to carry them out must be rationed. The same is true for the next levels down of high decision-makers; and lacking such detailed high-level intervention, we can almost count on the workings of the bureaucracy to make substantial changes in the outcomes desired by those who made the decisions. Ordinarily it is the Chiefs of Naval Operations and their subordinates who execute the plans. And, since the bureaucracies and parts of a bureaucracy are connected in series (there are no competing navies to act as alternative channels), it does not take many subordinates to foul the whole thing up.

This is why the business-market system is capable of working better; competing businesses are connected in parallel, and the failure of one does not mean the failure of the system. It is not clear that internal business operations are particularly different from government operations. Some of the major inflexibilities and bottlenecks frequently attributed to governmental operations are increasingly being reproduced in business. It is often argued, for example, that job tenure in civil service tends to protect the incapable and promote the cautious. But at least in big companies, it is not much easier to fire someone than it is in the civil service. It is contended that government bureaucracies tend to growth for the sake of growth, but Parkinson's Law was never applied just to public bureaucracies; it is just as applicable to private ones. One of the major flaws in public operations is supposed to be (and is, in fact) the elevation of precise accountability for public funds above all other principles. This is certainly true in public bureaucracy; but accountability for funds is really not much less stringent in most companies. The difference is that private firms have other distinguishable and superordinate objectives—the self-interest objectives of profit, survival, and growth in a competitive system—so that fund accountability is not dominant.

And this gets to the nature of the market system, based as it is on decentralized self-interest, rather than to the internal workings of business. Public bureaucracies do not ordinarily provide competition or alternative channels. Internal bureaucratic operations may be much the same in the private sector as in the public, but in virtually all fields of business endeavor in the United States alternative channels do exist within a product market, and there is some capability for the fittest to survive and prosper. Even in the automobile industry, a few competitors do help keep one another honest, and this tendency is assisted by the internal competition fostered by the manufacturing giants. Looked at from the viewpoint of the consumer, production facilities are connected in parallel, and even with only a few parallel channels, this makes all the difference in the world. For the most part, this differs from governmental bureaucratic practice, in which even though there may be multiple jurisdictions overlapping geographically (more than 1,000 have been counted in each of the New York and Los Angeles metropolitan areas), there is seldom any overlap in both geography and function simultaneously. In Southern California there is a Los Angeles city school system, a Los Angeles County school system, and a multitude of other systems, but the resident of any area has his choice of only one. It is possible that public bureaucratic systems might be connected more in parallel, that is, more competitively, than they are now, and it is possible that if this were to happen, they might pick up some of the advantages of business operations. This possibility is discussed further in the final part of this chapter.

Increased bureaucratic competition, however, is seldom suggested. Proposals for better planning and implementation of public programs ordinarily proceed along different and perhaps more classical lines. Most existing proposals can be grouped into two categories. The first of these contains those suggestions that would maintain the existing internal workings of bureaucracies: changing control, supervision, perhaps internal organization, but assuming the current structure of rules to be followed and bureaucrats to follow them because they are rules. The second category contains those ideas that would, on the basis of recent analysis of the internal workings of bureaucracy, try to restructure to improve the motivations of the bureaucrats. These categories overlap somewhat, but it is useful to illustrate them with a couple of examples from each.

One prototypical example of the first category, changing the control mechanisms while not tinkering too much with underlying structure, is provided by former Secretary of Housing and Urban Development Robert C. Wood. "What America needs," he says, "is a better bureaucracy, not less of one; discipline in bureaucracy, not amateurs run riot." [6] He recommends the federal government's making Cabinet officers the instruments of Presidential authority rather than the representatives of the bureaucracies they supervise, thus lessening the power of the Executive Office of the President; changing the outlook of bureaucracies; putting federal programs on a multiagency basis with a single "lead" agency in final authority; and synchronizing the budget and other schedules of the executive and legislative branches of the government. The second of these, changing the outlook of bureaucracies, would fall into the other category of proposals, working on the underlying structure, but Wood admits that he does not know how to go about it. The other three proposals clearly fall under the rubric of tinkering at the top. They might do something to improve the making of policy; they might improve the implementation of policy down to the level of assistant secretaries and bureau chiefs. But assistant secretaries and bureau chiefs carry out very few operations by themselves, and the continuation of series-connected bureaucratic operations below this level would guarantee that the outcomes would remain pretty much as they have been.

The proposal to give final authority to a lead agency, though also tinkering at the top, is somewhat more relevant to the subject matter here. Since it runs almost directly counter to the contentions of this chapter, it deserves more specific attention. Wood's proposal is designed to do away with the confusion and conflict that occur in public programs when it is not perfectly clear who is to rule what. No observer of the operations of such programs could deny this confusion. But the criterion used throughout this book for measuring programs is that of effectiveness in reaching desired objectives, and though it is tempting to suggest that doing away with chaos and confusion is a necessary condition for such effectiveness, this is not necessarily so. It is not necessarily so because the alternative to confusion—an alternative exemplified by Wood's lead agency idea—is operation of a public program by a single bureaucratic group monopolizing all the necessary authority, and once such a group has such a monopoly, it is subject to all the dangers discussed here, the dangers summarized as series-connected operation and operation by trying to set, interpret, and follow a set of rules. In addition, in the case of controversial social programs—and these are the ones Wood is most concerned with—monopolized operation by an established bureaucracy (for example, the kind of bureaucracy Wood ran as Secretary of HUD) means subjecting such a controversial program to the much less controversial and much better established ideologies and interests represented by the established bureaucracy. Since controversial programs are ordinarily set up to get around such ideologies and interests, monopolistic operation by an established bureaucracy is not likely to help.

In any case, the primary criticism of Wood can be summarized by saying that his prescriptions seem to change very little of what has failed to work in recent years. A more thoroughgoing attempt to achieve the same kind of objectives by changing things at the top was the program budgeting effort of the 1960s. In a way, program budgeting was the epitome of the attempt to do things better by doing them "right." That is, it was thought that by making program objectives explicit, setting side-by-side alternative means of reaching these objectives, and estimating effectiveness and costs of alternative public programs, public officials at all levels would be given the information necessary to choose and implement the best available programs. Given the information, they could then be expected to carry the programs through; little explicit attention was paid to implementation of the program budgeters' plans. Program budgeting was the high point of the effort to plan right and get the system to follow the plans. It did not work very well.

The history of program budgeting can be begun with its introduction into the Department of Defense during 1961. It has never been clear to what extent the initial major and desirable changes in American military policy made by Secretary McNamara and President Kennedy were the result of the new system rather than being the result of eight years of growth in the fallow intellectual fields of the Eisenhower administration. Many of the early Kennedy-McNamara decisions obviously predated the new decision systems of the Department of Defense; some decisions may have come out of the new system. In any case, in addition to the major changes in military force structure during 1961 and 1962, the new regime did put into the Department of Defense a new decision system that made the explicit objectives and instruments of military policy far clearer than they had been before. During the 1950s, the typical controversy within the Department of Defense had been over the division of the budget among the three services, and the typical outcome was to split the difference. During the 1960s, the subject of the controversy was much the same, but the debate was couched in terms of deterrent effect, military effectiveness, and the like. The ultimate decisions were also expressed and presumably made in these terms.

All this sounds quite good, yet its long-run effect may be rather meager. In the field of strategic weaponry, certainly major changes were made between the 1950s and 1960s, not only in the weaponry itself but in the basis for making decisions on these weapons. The new missiles—Minuteman and Polaris—came from the decision-making of the 1950s. But the decision to buy fewer missiles and spend more on protecting them was a new type of decision. Yet it is difficult to attribute these changes to the onset of program budgeting in the Defense Department as such. The results of sophisticated analysis they surely were, but such sophisticated analysis of clearly defined problems has always been possible and indeed has frequently even been done. The characteristic of the strategic weapons debates and decisions of the 1960s is that the problem was definable and, once a few parameters had been set, even calculable.

And even if we count the rationalization of the basis for strategic decisions as a triumph for clear planning over the bureaucratic split-the-difference method, it is a limited triumph; the same principles were never applied to anywhere near the same extent in decisions on general purpose forces. They were never applied because the problems were less clear-cut, less computable, and there were few cases in which such planning could be compelling enough to carry the day. Perhaps program budgeting made a difference in choice of tactical weapons; it may be argued that the choices were better and more rational than would have been the case without the planning. But the F-111 case—the choice of a fighter-bomber to be used jointly by Air Force and Navy—at least, argues otherwise. There are those who argue that the many problems of this weapons system were due to ignoring systematic planning in favor of politics rather than to a failure of such planning; either way, it suggests the limitations of the planning. In any case, after eight years, it certainly can be said that rational planning raised the intellectual level of the Pentagon; it is far less certain that it made any fundamental or lasting change in the making of military policy or in its execution by the military bureaucracy. Even under McNamara's Johnson administration successor, Clark Clifford, program budgeting lost some of its power. Under Nixon's Secretary of Defense Melvin Laird, it tended to disappear.

During 1965, however, McNamara was riding high and program budgeting looked good. For this reason, President Johnson directed that the system be generalized throughout the federal government. The results here were less mixed than in the defense case; in retrospect, it seems to have made very little difference. Where it did have an effect, the effect was incidental to the existence of the planning system itself, but for the most part it made very little dent on the bureaucratic way of doing things. For one thing, most federal agencies never really implemented program budgeting as it had been intended. They imposed a new nominal structure on the old way of making decisions, and they left it at that. For routine decisions, the new matrix may have made a difference, though it is difficult to say where. In a few agencies—notably the Department of Health, Education and Welfare and the Office of Economic Opportunity (OEO)—program budgeting was implemented seriously. Even here, however, though there was an effect, there were few major changes attributable to the new system. The new system worked to some extent in providing an input of rationality—an ability to explore costs, consequences, and alternatives—to decision-makers who wanted an input of rationality, but most decision-makers cared little for this sort of input or this sort of rationality, and they were perfectly capable of defeating it. And again because of the series connection of the bureaucracy, the failure to implement meant that the new systems had very little effect on the whole of government decision-making.

To take program budgeting in the OEO as an example (both because I am most familiar with it and because it is supposed to have been among the best), the first OEO program budget was prepared in 1965, even before the Johnson directive was promulgated. It was a program budget not merely for the $1.5 billion of the OEO, but for the $20 billion of programs that were considered to be part of the War on Poverty. This first budget was a distinct intellectual success. It was presented in successive briefings to Budget Director Charles Schultze, to Vice President Hubert Humphrey, and to Presidential Assistant Joseph Califano. Intellectually it was a triumph; unfortunately, it was proposed at a time when escalation in Vietnam tightened up available funds drastically, and at a time when the War on Poverty seemed to be becoming something of a political disaster to the administration, and the program budget had no effect on either the level or the allocation of funds made available to the War on Poverty that year or any other subsequent year. One might blame this on the special circumstances of the military escalation and politics; since the contention here, however, is not that rational planning is internally inconsistent, but that it does not work well in a world of bureaucracy, politics, and so on, the fact of its failure at OEO is quite relevant.

The failure was not complete. Analysis done at OEO under the program budget rubric did affect policy, occasionally even in a major way, but these effects were specific and partial. OEO planning analysis, for example, was a vital factor in the series of activities that culminated in President Nixon's proposal for radical changes in the U.S. welfare system. Starting in 1965, the planning office was inclined toward a federal "negative income tax" as a substitute for the existing confused federal-state-local welfare structure. Considerable analysis was done on various payment schemes and their costs under various assumptions about the distribution of income, and it was discovered that the crucial missing piece of data was any evidence of the effect of income maintenance on the incentives to work of recipients. To obtain this information, an experiment was set up in New Jersey during 1968. Then during January 1969, at the beginning of the Nixon administration, presidential adviser Daniel Moynihan was able, for various political and other reasons, to sell the President on the idea of drastically changing the welfare system. The previous analysis and evidence on the negative income tax was available and, in spite of the fact that Moynihan himself favored a quite different scheme, the availability of the negative income tax analysis made this the plan that he, and ultimately the administration, supported.

A second example is provided by analysis of manpower programs. During 1967, the administration put together a package of training and employment programs for the worst urban slum areas under the title "Concentrated Employment Program." At the time this was done, however, OEO, on the basis of its analysis, insisted on tabling doubts about the viability of such a program that failed to provide funds to sweeten the pot for business to provide training and jobs. This was duly noted and initially ignored by the administration, but when it became clear through the year that the Concentrated Employment Program was not working well, in large measure because of lack of business commitment, and when at the beginning of the election year of 1968 President Johnson wanted a program with business appeal, the analysis behind the program of federal subsidies to business for job training was available. It became the basis of the administration's Job Opportunities in the Business Sector (JOBS) program.

The implication of these two examples is that rational analysis and planning on specific ideas can become immensely valuable when the time has come politically for a specific idea that might be provided by such analysis. Other similar examples could be taken from the program evaluation end of program budgeting analysis. A relatively negative evaluation report on the Johnson-initiated Head Start program was available, for instance, at a time when the new Nixon administration wanted a case on which it could criticize the way the old administration had done business. But in each of these cases, the analysis was specific and was useful because its time had come; the relevance of the system of program budgeting was only that it provided a cover operation for doing analysis of a kind that could have been done anyway and indeed had always been done to some extent within the federal government.

And this is the point: Program budgeting at its best improved the system a bit; it changed nothing fundamentally. What improvements there were appeared in particularly amenable areas of the decision-making system, but program implementation went virtually unchanged. All this is quite consistent with the retrospective study of program budgeting written by

Charles Schultze, the Director of the Budget Bureau who initiated the new system in 1965.[7] Schultze defends program budgeting essentially as an input of rationality into a decision-making system that needed all the rationality it could get, and he claims no systemic changes. But of course this is retrospective; at least the 1965 public statements of the President and of Schultze himself indicated hope for much more.

However, the system of planning and implementing policy has not been changed fundamentally. Why not? Several reasons can be assigned:

1. The science of analytical planning has not developed to the point where rational arguments are so compelling that they must perforce sweep all before them. Strong advocates of positions opposed to those of the analysts are always able to find flaws in the "rational" argument and to exploit these flaws. The 1968–1969 evaluation, which cast doubt on the effectiveness of the Head Start program in improving the learning capabilities of its enrollees, for example, had a number of limitations. For one thing, the constraints of time meant that long-run improvements in learning capabilities would not show up during the term of the study; for another, the limitations of statistical method in a large-scale program made it impossible to create a perfect control group. And third, the evaluation looked only at learning gain, which, though it was the central objective of Head Start, was not the only one. As a result, the evaluative case against Head Start was never airtight. As Walter Williams and John Evans point out, those who favored expansion of Head Start were able to use the study's gaps and limitations in a campaign to discredit it entirely, a campaign that ultimately engaged both *The New York Times'* education columnist Fred Hechinger and Secretary of Health, Education and Welfare Robert Finch. Even though the study in question is one of the best of its type, both in method and scope, it was not and could not have been flawless, and the inevitable flaws strongly limited its effectiveness in changing policy.[8]

2. Most programs are not as readily analyzable as Head Start anyhow, because in most cases, data for program analysis

are either completely unavailable or are of extremely poor quality. Social programs of the type under discussion are necessarily carried out in detail in the thousands of places where the people needing the program are located. Those who operate the programs are concerned primarily just with operating them, and to the extent that they are concerned with data at all, it is only with the data necessary for their particular operations. Time and time again, federal agencies at the top have tried to impose nation-wide data systems; they have always failed. They have failed because of the very limited possibility of forcing the operating bureaucrats to provide data in which they were not interested and because of the complete impossibility of forcing them to make the data accurate. A typical example, noted above, was the attempt of OEO's Community Action Program to obtain information from the thousand local agencies throughout the country. The paradox that was never solved was that the simplest data system that could be designed was far more complicated than the most complex that could be executed in the field. To some extent, operational data collection for specific purposes is possible. In the case of the Head Start evaluation, special testing of a selected sample of children was carried out, for example. But this reinforces the idea that pieces of additional rational analysis are possible; routine carrying out of systematic program planning as was hoped for from the program budgeting effort requires massive and continuing data, and this is not possible.

3. Finally, for program budgeting to have worked would have required planning and analysis personnel not merely in Washington but at every bureaucratic level, and personnel in anywhere near this number were simply not available, nor were they likely to be. Even in Washington itself, the few agencies that took program budgeting seriously had major difficulties in finding people. And this was in spite of the fact that their reputation for doing good analytical work made them very attractive to the kinds of people needed. Had the effort been extended as broadly throughout the federal government as its instigators had hoped, the shortage of personnel in all agencies might have crippled the system completely. Insofar as deepening the effort

below the very top Washington staffs is concerned, this was always impossible.

The last point in particular gets to the main reason why the program budgeting kind of proposal is never likely to provide more than a marginal addition of rationality into the bureaucratic way of doing business: because the rule-giving and interpreting mode of doing business in bureaucracy and the series connection of those trying to follow the rules would require program planners as well as implementers who understand program planning at every level to convert program budgeting into a major structural change, and such people are not available nor are they ever likely to be. Even if they were, it probably would not work because people of this nature are rather likely to be bright and innovative, and innovative interpretation of the rules is not what is needed.

All this leads to the second class of proposals for changing bureaucracies. This category contains those suggestions that, starting with an understanding of the way things really work within a bureaucratic organization, would utilize this knowledge to make them work better. The informing characteristic of such ideas is that behind the formal structure of relationships in a bureaucracy is an informal structure that may be quite different and is much more relevant than the formal one to causation in bureaucratic operations. This concept is not new; it goes back at least to the Hawthorne Western Electric experiments of Elton Mayo during the 1920s, and was picked up, systematized, and magnified by Argyris during the 1940s.[9] Much of the early work was more descriptive than prescriptive, but there has always been a thread of attempted change in the work, and this is very strong currently. One of the major current subschools is that of Organization Development, the ethos of which is well described in a short study by one of its leaders, Warren Bennis, of the University of Buffalo:

This book rests on three basic propositions: The first is an evolutionary hypothesis that every age develops an organizational form most appropriate to the genius of that age and that certain unparalleled changes are taking place which make it necessary to revitalize and rebuild our organizations. The second is that the only viable way to change organizations is to change their "culture," that is, to change the systems within which people work and live. A "culture" is a way of life, a system of beliefs and values, an accepted form of interaction and relating. Changing individuals, while terribly important, cannot yield the fundamental impact so necessary for the revitalization and renewal I have in mind—if our organizations are to survive and develop. Thirdly, a new *social* awareness is required by people in organizations along with its spiritual ancestor, *self*-awareness. Organizations are becoming collectively aware of their destiny and their path to guiding their destiny. This proposition asserts that social consciousness is more difficult to induce than personal awareness but more essential in the kind of world we are living in.[10]

Though Organization Development is not the only approach in this school of thought, the quotation is typical enough for current purposes. The effort is a serious one, but because changing the "culture" of the bureaucracy, that is, changing the motivations of people or the ways these motivations are translated into operations, would be a Herculean task as applied to the public bureaucracy as a whole, the Organization Development group and others of this general school provide advice that can only be utilized at the level of detailed operation. The prescriptions may be excellent; my background gives me no way to judge, but they look good. Nonetheless, as applied to restructuring the public bureaucracies of the United States, they bring us back to the law of large numbers and the black boxes connected in series. For if the top managers at the level being discussed here were to try to develop their next level of managers by use of the prescriptions of the developers, and the next level developed the next, and so on down the line, there would inevitably be falloff and misinterpretation, and the strength of the chain would again be that of the weak links. To impose Organization Development from the top on such a structure would be little different from imposing any other set of rules on bureaucracy, and it is this kind of imposition that characterizes the failure of public bureaucracy. Indeed, in this particular case, the public sector may have drawbacks compared to the private one beyond even the drawbacks of series connection as compared to parallel connection. The strength and sanctity of tenure in the civil service, for example, may make it very difficult to change the culture of the bureaucracy. In addition, some of the underlying rules governing the current bureaucracy (the supreme importance of fund accountability, for example) would also make it quite difficult to reacculturate the system. It might be argued, and in fact it has frequently been argued, that such accountability for public funds ought to be considered of less importance than it is. But to achieve this we would have not merely to change the culture of the bureaucracy but the political culture of the nation.

None of this is to argue that Organization Development or the other approaches in the category are worthless for public bureaucracies. Even an instruction from the top to read some of the relevant books might be of some assistance, and perhaps utilization of some of the arcane arts of what might be called sociotherapy (parallel to psychotherapy) might help. But it is quite clear that at this point nobody has an answer that can be systematically imposed throughout public bureaucracies by those who are trying to design public policies that can be implemented. If such an answer existed, it might turn this book around; it seems not to exist.

Since it seems impossible, at least at this point in time, to change overall public bureaucratic systems substantially either by changing their direction at the top by such devices as program budgeting, or by changing their culture a la Organization Development, it may be useful to look for a third class of solutions, less ideal but perhaps more workable than the others. What is suggested here is less ideal in the sense that even if it worked very well, this would be less well than program budgeting or Organization Development if they worked well. But the contention here is that in the real world this alternative concept is substantially more likely to work at all.

The concept, which might be termed "competitive bureaucracy," can be applied by the top levels of officials as in the case of program budgeting, but the application is much more consistent with the way bureaucracies really operate than that of program budgeting. The concept recognizes that insofar as top-level decision-makers and planners are concerned, bureaucratic units are black boxes that had best not be tinkered with. The black boxes ought not to be tinkered with internally, but it is possible to tinker with the relationships among them, in other words, to treat bureaucratic units (small bureaucracies) as closed subsystems and try to affect their workings by changing the connections between them and the external stimuli.

Specifically, what might work and by some evidence does work is trying to treat bureaucratic units as if they were competing business units. From the point of view of the top public policy-maker, business units are also black boxes whose actions are to be affected from the outside as in the cases of the workings of business cycle policy and some of the other examples of Chapter 3. But the advantage of the business system to the public official is that the boxes are connected in parallel; so, perhaps, might be the black boxes of bureaucracy.

If it is possible to change the workings of public bureaucracy, it may be through competition. The analogy between business units and bureaucratic units is not a precise one. Profits provide business with a relatively clear criterion of success not available to public bureaucracies, and in the public case the influence of the citizenry on success must be expressed more directly than the consumer's influence in the private market. Nonetheless, there is reason to believe that competition in fact can stimulate public bureaucracies to more effective performance on public policy.

Evidence of the success of bureaucratic competition does not abound, simply because such competition, being antithetical to the bureaucratic ethos (competition = overlap, duplication, and so on), does not abound. Nonetheless, examples do exist, and these examples do seem to show a degree of stimulation not typical of bureaucratic operations.

In the military sphere, for example, the services do overlap, and where this happens, the cost-effectiveness of military capabilities seems higher than in the areas where there is either unchallenged single-service monopoly or multiservice cooperation. The evidence is necessarily impressionistic, but it is illustrative.

A major area of service overlap, for example, is in the purchase and utilization of fighter aircraft, and the contrast
between a competitive and noncompetitive example here seems
instructive. During the early 1960s, the Air Force and Navy
both developed similar fighter-bombers: the Air Force F-105,
produced by Republic Aviation, and the Navy F-4, produced
by McDonnell. There is no doubt that these craft were competitive; they were similar planes with similar functions, and both
the services and the producers competed to have them used
throughout the military air arms. The F-4 won, and, in spite of
its reluctance to use a Navy-developed plane, the Air Force did
adopt the F-4, which became a major weapon in Vietnam for
both services. The F-105 also was used in Vietnam and per-
formed in a highly satisfactory manner; the contrast here is not
between these two planes, but between their competitive case
and the noncompetitive development of the F-111 (called the
TFX when it was under development) for the two services. The
design of the F-111 was competitive on the industry side (Con-
vair-Fort Worth ultimately got the contract for reasons that
have been the subject of massive debate), but on the bureaucratic side, which is the matter of concern here, competition did
not exist. The Air Force and the Navy, under the watchful eyes
of the Department of Defense, worked together on the F-111.
Plenty of disagreement existed, but it was thrashed out and a
decision come to, rather than doing it both ways, as would have
happened with competition. And the final aircraft became perhaps the most striking military hardware failure of the 1960s;
the Navy version was ultimately not produced, while the Air
Force version has had some difficulty keeping its wings on. The
contrast to the F-4 versus F-105 case is quite striking.

And, indeed, other military evidence bears out the same hypothesis. Strategic missile systems have been a major subject of
Air Force–Navy rivalry; both the Minuteman and Polaris seem
to be highly effective weapon systems. (At least they have
clearly served their deterrent purpose thus far.) In World War
II, the Army and the Marine Corps were rivals to some extent
over amphibious warfare; both the Marines' Pacific and the
Army's European landings were carried out very well. On the

other hand, returning to recent hardware, military transport aircraft are not competitive bureaucratically; neither are tanks.
And two major cases in point in Congressional questioning of
military procurement have been the C-5A transport and the
Army's Main Battle Tank.

The evidence is admittedly selective, but it is real. A truism
among military planners is that the real enemy is not a foreign
nation but a "friendly" fellow service, a statement most frequently made as a joke. But because competiton is not ordinarily considered to be a natural mode for bureaucracies, interservice rivalry is frowned on; yet without such rivalry, it seems
likely that the military position of the United States would be
much poorer than it is.

In the fields of domestic policy, bureaucratic competition is
nothing new; President Franklin Roosevelt was a past master of
using this technique of manipulation to gain his ends. More recently, a number of examples of the benefits of bureaucratic
competition can be taken from the experiences of the War on
Poverty in which the Office of Economic Opportunity was created as a stimulus and a goad to old-line agencies in a much
more deliberate manner than is ordinarily the case. The creation of OEO as a direct operating agency by the Economic Opportunity Act of 1964 was uniformly decried by the existing
agencies, each of which had a mandate in a field of endeavor
covered by OEO.[11] Yet in spite of the fact that the bureaucratic
competition hurt and hurt badly, the leader of one of the bureaucracies challenged, Secretary of Labor Willard Wirtz, was
able to testify before a Congressional committee in 1967:

I know the argument that some of these programs are now at a
point that we should shift them someplace else. I am in a pretty
good position to say to you, Mr. Chairman, that it takes more than
three years to upset the inertial forces that characterize the Department of Labor. Three years is not enough as a basis for any assumption that the established departments are now going to do
right what they didn't do at all before. I would urge very, very
strongly the continued development of this program for the time
being through somebody whose job and whose sole job is to recognize the effects of poverty and to develop those institutions and

procedures which will meet that problem. There will be a time for turning it over, but it is not now.[12]

Mr. Wirtz said this under some pressure from the White House; nonetheless, it rings true and basically is true. Indeed, in an entirely voluntary summary of some of the battles he had participated in as the Labor Department's chief proponent of protecting manpower programs from the annoying competitive influence of OEO's Community Action Program, former Assistant Secretary of Labor Stanley Ruttenberg wrote in 1970 that:

> All during the period of the development of manpower programs for the disadvantaged, there was a continuing struggle between the Office of Economic Opportunity and the Department of Labor over the role of the state Employment Service agencies and the Community Action agencies vis-á-vis manpower programs. The Employment Service cause was championed with great fervor by the Bureau of Employment Security. Ardent CAA support came from the Community Action Program division of OEO. Both sides recognized the importance of manpower in the nascent drive for community development. Both correctly saw manpower as the key to control and power in the urban ghetto areas. Each time the struggle came to a head—as it did repeatedly—it was resolved by a series of compromises that tried to give a part of the action to both groups. There were always, of course, individual staff members in both agencies who felt that their side was being sold out. But it was always my feeling that there was, and is, a legitimate role for both the Employment Service and the CAAs. If the Employment Service is to become the chief operating arm of national manpower policy, as I think it must, then it must change its attitudes and practices. But it could not, and will not, change to meet the needs of the disadvantaged without constant pressure to force such a change. Part of the pressure can come from the Community Action agencies which—despite their limitations—effectively voice the aspirations of the poor. In 1967 the CAAs were developing a capability of reaching the disadvantaged that the Employment Service did not have. Therefore, I saw the two agencies as complementing each other, in a constructive competition that could result in better service to those who needed it.[13]

This is a striking statement from someone whose chief problem as Assistant Secretary for Manpower was to keep the OEO out of his hair. And the examples go far beyond manpower.

The Head Start preschool program challenged educational institutions; in Washington and throughout the country, they responded (not uniformly, but they responded) by at least paying more attention to the problems of deprived children. Health institutions, including the federal H of the Department of HEW, responded to the challenge of OEO health programs, and so on down the line.

The potential for such outside stimuli to improve the workings of self-satisfied bureaucrats is another aspect of one of the modes of nonbureaucratic execution of public programs discussed in Chapter 3. It was suggested there that one substitute for detailed bureaucratic administration of programs was the releasing and directing of political forces that would tend to move things in a desired direction. The chief current example was the Community Action Program which, by aiding the poor in urban slums and ghettos to become a political force in their own right, enabled them to move local policy substantially more toward an antipoverty stance than would otherwise have been possible. Chapter 3 viewed this phenomenon from outside the bureaucracy; from inside, what was happening in almost every American city of any size was that local bureaucracies, feeling pushed and challenged by these forces of the poverty community, did in fact change their operations in ways that did substantially more and better on behalf of the poor. State Employment Service offices, which had been located in downtown areas, moved out into the slums where people needed the jobs; this was an effect of the OEO pressure at the national level as well as the local pressure of Community Action. School boards began to pay much more attention to the needs of poor and minority students, welfare authorities to the feelings of their clients.

I have discussed and documented this elsewhere.[14] The point here, however, is that under the stimulus of pushing and competition from the outside, many bureaucracies did in fact change their ways. This is not to say that competitive stimulation is a panacea; it is not. But for many public programs and policies, particularly in such areas as manpower, housing, and poverty programs in general, bureaucratic competition may complement programs that bypass the bureaucracy to bring about substantially more satisfactory program results than seem available in any other way.

Given the bureaucratic ethos, in which competition becomes duplication and is thus to be shunned, this conclusion may be surprising. But, given the knowledge we have from various studies of bureaucracy, it should not be. The picture of bureaucracy and of bureaucrats that emerges from recent work is one in which action (or inaction) is impelled by a mixture of motives: some personal, ranging from conservative preservation of status and stability to activist seeking for advancement; some outside the self, ranging from preservation of the organization to fulfilling national objectives. Except for the most extreme cases, each bureaucrat is motivated by a mixture of these, and it would be futile to try to discover the national average of motives for bureaucrats. What does seem to be true, however, is that for almost every sort of bureaucratic motivation, the continued good health of the organization—the bureaucratic agency—is close to central. An exception may be the ultra-idealistic motivation that leads a bureaucrat not only to put national objectives in the supreme position but also to make his own interpretation of national objectives that sole touchstone, as when State Department Security Officer Otto Otepka went over the head of the Department to make his point with Congressional committees, or former bureaucrat Daniel Ellsberg released without authorization papers he had obtained through his bureaucratic position. With this sort of exception, however, even the idealist looks at his agency as the chosen instrument for attaining his goals, whether relatively idealistic or more personal, such as security or advancement. And this is the reason that the competitive challenge to an organization is likely to be a stimulus. Whether the individual motive is personal security, personal advancement, or impersonal objectives, a competitive threat to the organization is likely to cause the organization and its members to perform differently in reaction to the challenge because they value the organization. If a different performance is better (by the standards of the top policy-maker), the challenge has worked. If different is poorer, the status of the organization and its members will suffer; they will have to react further or suffer further.

The question for the policy-makers, then, is what kind of competitive stimulus to what kind of bureaucratic organization will work best. For, though competition, both in the market-place and in bureaucracy, has a good track record, its success is by no means certain. When competitors are few in number, as frequently happens in the market and almost always in the bu-reaucracy, they tend to collusion and/or oligopoly; this is one possible reaction to the challenge. Collusion is the explicit agreement to compete lightly or not at all in order to avoid the insecurities the firm faces in the marketplace; economic theory has shown that with few enough firms, there is no need for ex-plicit collusion because oligopolistic firms can recognize their own interests in not competing too hard. And such a failure to compete very hard defeats the public interest in competition. In consumer markets it means that prices will not go so low as they should. More important here, it means that consumers will not have the variety of choice that competition should supply. In consumer markets, however, some degree of competition is preserved, at least in the United States, because both the mar-ket ethos and the antitrust laws make collusion difficult and the appearance of collusion questionable. Even in industries with very few firms, such as automobiles, a major degree of real competition is preserved.

Because the bureaucratic ethos is precisely the opposite of the market ethos, however (far from being a desideratum, com-petition is a waste), fostering bureaucratic competition in the face of the natural tendency toward oligopoly is more difficult. What may help here are some of the distinctions among types of bureaucrats and organizations drawn by the analysts of bu-reaucracy. Downs, for example, distinguishes among bureau-cratic "conservers" and "climbers." [15] The former are moti-vated primarily by security considerations, the latter by advancement. By the very definition of the terms, climbers want change, conservers, stability; it follows that the policy-maker desiring change should stress organizations dominated by climbers, the policy-maker wanting stability should stress the conservers.

It would further follow that old organizations are conserver dominated, new ones will attract climbers because of the potentiality for rapid advancement. So the policy-maker wanting change through competition has the best chance of achieving such change by creating new organizations to carry it out. The new organizations will attract climbers (and, incidentally, attract bureaucrats dedicated to the new policies being promoted) and are likely to work effectively at least for a while. More important, perhaps, the climbers will put the new organization into a position of competing with the old, and the challenge may change the performance of the conserver-dominated old organization in the desired direction. This is the evidence of the OEO examples cited above, and the theories of the bureaucratic analysts go a long way toward explaining the evidence.

The lesson, then, is that bureaucratic operations can be made more effective through competition, and competition can be promoted within a bureaucracy by the frequent creation of the new to challenge the old. Two caveats need mention, however. The first is the obvious one that if the policy-maker desires stability rather than change, he should go with the old. (If the contention is correct that bureaucracies are inherently inefficient, however, even the conservative policy-maker will want change in order to promote effectiveness in reaching the old objectives.) And the second warning, perhaps also obvious, is that the new grows old, so that after some period of time (three years? five years?), the new, grown old, will need its own challenges.

In any case, bureaucratic competiton has important uses, just as does the utilization of market and political competition for public programs. The utility of bureaucratic competition clearly applies to federal programs; it seems quite applicable to such locally controlled programs as primary and secondary education, where a prerequisite for the improvement of school programs is a challenge to school boards and school administrators who are satisfied with doing things in the good old ways. The competitive idea cannot be applied everywhere; it would seem difficult, for example, to compete with draft boards or tax assessors. Nonetheless, it may be a very important part of a restructured policy system.

The next two chapters, then, review the troops and pick up the pieces. Chapter 7 summarizes the implications thus far for policy-making; the final chapter, the implications for future policy study.

Notes

1. James G. March and Herbert A. Simon, *Organizations* (New York: Wiley, 1958).
2. Anthony Downs, *Inside Bureaucracy,* A Rand Corporation Research Study (Boston: Little, Brown, 1967).
3. Richard E. Neustadt, *Presidential Power* (New York: Wiley, 1960).
4. Michel Crozier, *The Bureaucratic Phenomenon* (Chicago: University of Chicago Press, 1964).
5. Graham T. Allison, *Essence of Decision: Explaining the Cuban Missile Crisis* (Boston: Little, Brown, 1971).
6. Robert C. Wood, "When Government Works," *The Public Interest,* (Winter 1970): 40.
7. Charles L. Schultze, *The Politics and Economics of Public Spending* (Washington, D.C.: The Brookings Institution, 1969).
8. Walter Williams and John W. Evans, "The Politics of Evaluation: The Case of Head Start," in *Evaluating the War on Poverty,* ed. L. A. Ferman and R. D. Lambert, Annals of the American Academy of Political and Social Science (Philadelphia, 1969).
9. See, for example, Christopher Argyris, *Personality and Organization: The Conflict Between the System and the Individual* (New York: Harper & Row, 1957).
10. Warren G. Bennis, *Organization Development: Its Nature, Origins, and Prospects* (Boston: Addison-Wesley, 1969).
11. See, for example, James L. Sundquist, *Politics and Policy: The Eisenhower, Kennedy and Johnson Years* (Washington: Brookings Institution, 1968), pp. 111–154.
12. Economic Opportunity Act amendments of 1967, Hearings before the Committee on Education and Labor, House of Representatives, 90th Congress, First Session on HR 8311, part II, pp. 1193–1194 (Washington, D.C.: General Printing Office, 1967).
13. Stanley H. Ruttenberg, *Manpower Challenge of the 1970s: Institutions and Social Change* (Baltimore: Johns Hopkins Press, 1970), pp. 54–55.
14. Robert A. Levine, *The Poor Ye Need Not Have with You: Lessons from the War on Poverty* (Cambridge: M.I.T. Press, 1970), pp. 165–167.
15. Downs, *Inside Bureaucracy,* pp. 92 ff.

7

Applications: The Planning and Implementation of Public Programs

MOST PUBLIC PROGRAMS fail to produce results that meet the reasonable expectations of their planners. They fail because planners and policy-makers cannot determine in advance the applications of a given policy to all possible situations; discretion must be left to those who carry out the policy. But discretion necessarily includes the right to be wrong by the lights of policy-makers, and in terms of policy objectives the sum of such discretion most frequently comes out wrong. The typical bureaucratic attempt has been to correct this by proliferating rules to guide discretion; the dilemma is that the impossibility of advance determination of application means that the rules themselves must be interpreted through discretion.

What is needed, then, are systems in which operating instrumentalities respond to policy intentions. They must either respond in a precise nondiscretionary way, in which case what is called for is a highly centralized system, perhaps a computerized one. Or, the instrumentalities must respond to policy in a way such that discretion follows the intentions of the policy-makers. The latter statement covers almost all interesting policy questions; how to go about carrying out policies of this type is still an unsolved problem.

The previous chapters have presented and discussed evidence indicating that the discretionary systems most likely to work are those in which the discretion of the interpreters is guided not by rules for decision-making based on conceptions of the public interest, but rather by the self-interests of the interpreters. Self-interest can then be guided in the direction desired by policy through the adjustment of incentives. Three means of carrying through such a self-interest system have been suggested:

1. The use of economic market mechanisms, utilizing profit incentives to move the systems in the desired directions. It has been stressed here that the important element is the use of the market, not the use of business as such. As has been suggested, individual firms—at least large ones—have many of the same undesirable characteristics as public bureaucracies; it is the more or less competitive market that makes things work.

2. The economic market principle is not universally applicable. In particular, it is not applicable to the carrying out of policies concerning the distribution of economic and political resources. A somewhat similar mode that may be utilized here is the structuring of political forces so that these forces, acting in their own self-interest, will help change distribution of income or power in the direction desired by public policy. This means the supplementation of traditional economic markets with political bargaining markets.

3. Both of the first two modes are extragovernmental in the sense that policy is carried out by individuals, firms, or groups responsible to themselves and their own interests rather than to some higher loyalty. Nonetheless, many public functions will inevitably have to be carried out by public officials and employees responsible ultimately to an electorate. Thus, a public bureaucratic structure will remain, and the third mode of operation suggested has been to induce within bureaucracies competitive quasimarket or political situations in order to improve performance through competition.

The question now is which modes apply to what kinds of public systems and how? To examine this, it is useful initially to bisect the continuum of public policy-making that extends from the initial conception of a policy to its ultimate carrying out. In one category we can put the making of policy; in the other, its implementation.

Policy-Making and Planning

The making of public policy can in turn be divided conceptually between determining where we want to go on the one hand and planning (defined as the advance laying out of courses to get there) on the other. These two functions are, of course, closely intertwined, but they can be conceptually separated. The former—determining where to go—is clearly a public function. In a democracy, it is a political function, though in principle, it might be possible to use economic markets to "buy and sell" objectives. If two objectives, x and y, are competitive, it might be possible for those wanting x to pay those wanting y enough money to compensate for the latter's giving up objective y or at least giving up some portion of it. This is unlikely, however, particularly because of considerations of income distribution. Democracy means one man-one vote, not one dollar-one vote, and given unequal income distribution such a system for buying and selling objectives would be unworkable, if not intolerable. In addition, difficulties would arise in compensating groups as well as individuals.

For such reasons as this, the political marketplace substitutes for the economic one in determining where public policy is to go. The mechanism of the political marketplace is either referendum or representation, more typically and more successfully the latter. Typically, elected decision-makers are given the responsibility for determining where public policy should take us. But "where we want to go" is in itself a slurring concept. Does it mean, "Where do we want to get?" or does it mean "In what direction do we want to go?" This is where planning—the laying out in advance of courses—rejoins decision-making conceptually. An implication of this study has been that "where we want to get," setting future states as objectives and laying out courses to reach these objectives, has not worked and is indeed unworkable. It has not worked because laying out the course to an objective means detailing steps of policy execution not likely to be carried out in the desired way. This is a question again of the dilemma of human discretion and interpretation with its infinite richness and infinite potential for going wrong in a series-connected system.

Rather, the contention here is that we need a new sort of planning. Rather than selecting desirable future states and laying out courses over deceptive terrain, both policy-making and policy planning should be directional. That is, policy-makers should decide what general sort of future would be better than an alternative, and policy planners should lay out steps that show a probability of moving in that general direction. This concept of decision-making and planning, then, means starting from where we are—analysis of what will happen under current policies—as a baseline for possible policy change. It means perturbing of forces, such as incentives and political balances, so that the sum of the forces will move in directions more desirable to decision-makers than alternative directions. It means trial-and-error iteration of policies; if a planned step moves in a direction other than the expected one, it can be corrected. It means the resetting of profit incentives as in the case of business cycle policy, in which firms are induced to spend less or more by public actions that change the profit result of spending less or more. It means resetting of political balances as in the NLRA and CAP cases. It means competition designed to reset bureaucratic balances.

In each case, it is possible to change back and forth as contextual conditions change, as desires of policy-makers change, as policies work in unexpected ways. If the setting of profit incentives has caused inflation, it is possible to reset them to deflate. If the Wagner Act swung the balance to labor further than desired by the legislature, it was possible to correct the balance with the Taft-Hartley Act.

Much public planning in the past has been meaningless to the policy-maker because it has failed to tell him how to move in the desired direction as well as (or instead of) telling him that he should move that way because of the shimmering golden master-planned city to be approached. Urban planning has typically been of the shimmering city type and for that reason has been largely useless. Real planning must be of the how variety, and this is necessarily directional planning.

Even if the making of policy as such is necessarily a public function in a democracy, planning could in principle be public or private. That is, it ought to be possible for the policy-maker to choose a direction and for a completely objective hired analyst to then lay out steps that move in that direction. In practice, however, there is such a close intertwining of public policy-making and planning—an interplay between desirability and feasibility—that good public planners are in fact policy-makers and policy-makers must in part be planners. The close relationship of planning to the making of policy, however, implies that at least the central aspects of public planning, those most intimately connected with policy-making as such, must also be public. It would not do for an elected official to have to depend on private groups to tell him how to get where he wants to go. This does not mean that private planning inputs are not useful or important; it means that public planners responsible to elected officals are necessary to receive, interpret, and supplement such private inputs.

But planning itself is a public system subject to the same dangers of badly used discretion as other such systems. Bureaucratic planning can be as unsuccessful as bureaucratic anything else. And, of the three modes of reform—market, political competition among interest groups, and bureaucratic competition—the first, the use of money incentives to induce good planning, is inapplicable if planners are necessarily politically responsible public people. In large measure, the second mode, the explicit politicization of planning, is also impossible because planning does take some expertise. The laying out of courses with a substantial possibility that even the first steps will move matters in the desired direction is a skilled process not really appropriate for direct political or citizen participation. (This does not mean, of course, that hired planners cannot be responsive to the objectives of citizen groups in the same way as public planners are responsive to the objectives of elected officials. It merely means that the planning itself is too technical for every man to be his own planner.)

If the market and interest group political bargaining modes are not directly applicable to planning, however, public officials to whom planners report must be very careful to carry out the third mode, to deliberately induce and promote bureaucratic conflict. Planners should not be allowed to get too secure because planning can become ossified doctrine as easily as anything else, perhaps more easily. This has happened to a great extent in city planning and in military planning; predictably, it will happen to program budgeting, and indeed the early symptoms are already observable. For this reason, public planners and planning groups must constantly be challenged from outside the group, and because of the centrality of such public planning, the challenge is more important here than anywhere else.

The implication of all the above, however, is that though a distinction can be drawn between policy-making and policy execution, and planning is part of policy-making, planning for implementation is crucial. Planning is meaningless unless it is planning for carrying out policies. That is why even though this book has concentrated most of its discussion on systems for implementing policy, it is still a book about planning.

Policy Implementation

How, then, can planning be focused on the implementation of policy? Again, some distinctions are needed, this time among types of programs to be implemented. The key distinction is whether the objective of the implementation of a particular program is to carry out public policy as effectively as possible, that is, to accomplish a given task for the least resource cost and with the least distortion of the total economy, or whether it is to distribute resources, that is, goods, services, dollars, power, among parts of the population in a policy-determined pattern.

In economic terms, the distinction is close to that between allocation and distribution. Allocation is the parceling out of resources to produce a given bundle of products or results; the optimal allocation is one that produces the bundle using the smallest amount of resources or produces the largest bundle for a given amount of resources. Distribution, as has been discussed, is the parceling out of command over resources for consumption or other purposes to consuming units or to population groups; the optimal distribution is whatever policy says it is.

Some government programs have as a primary objective accomplishing a particular task in the most efficient way, and this implies the most efficient allocation of resources; some programs are designed explicitly to alter distribution of command over resources. Though most cases are mixed, containing elements of both allocation and distribution, a few are almost pure. The public objective of the postal system, for example, is to get the mail delivered most efficiently and at least cost. Money transfer payments, on the other hand, have an objective that can be defined as purely distributive.

For those programs where the stress is on efficient allocation, the evidence of this study indicates that market-like mechanisms are most useful. Where the efficiency desired is economic efficiency, economic market mechanisms will work best. Where the efficiency is a political efficiency—carrying out a task with the least squawk, for example—the political-bargaining mechanism seems most appropriate. For programs where a major objective is one of distribution, however, the economic market mechanism is less appropriate. As has been seen, the one thing the market does worst is to hand out its rewards according to a socially desired pattern. In some instances, the political-bargaining mechanism is appropriate for distributive programs; in other cases it is necessary to fall back on bureaucracy.

Thus, the continuum from market to bureaucracy is parallel in some sense to the continuum from efficiency objectives to distributive ones. Some qualifications are necessary, however. For one thing, the use of force must be mainly a public monopoly. Even though national defense comes as close as any case to having an objective definable in efficiency terms rather than distributive ones, the need for a public monopoly of force implies that defense is going to be a bureaucratic function. So for the most part will be the police function; so, for other reasons, will be many regulatory functions. In each of these cases, the overriding need for direct public monopoly or control leads to a corresponding need for public operation. As will be noted below, in the case of regulation this does not necessarily mean that the detailed workings of the system must be public, though this will be necessary in many cases.

In addition to the above qualifications of the principle of efficiency as a market function, and distribution as a public function, there must be a central and crucial qualification to the way the principle is applied. This is due to the fact that most distributive programs are complex enough in their execution that, even though resource redistribution is the objective, efficiency remains an important consideration. Many public housing and health programs, for example, have as their intention the redistributive function of providing better housing, health care, and the like to those at the lower end of the income distribution who cannot afford these out of their private incomes. But the provision of housing and health care is complicated enough that if done very inefficiently (as is frequently the case), it might best not be done at all.

Programs like this, with objectives that are primarily redistributive but with operations that require some degree of program efficiency, are the most frequent and important among public programs with social objectives. Thus, the mode of their implementation may be the most important question of all for public policy planning. What is suggested here, then, is that for these mixed cases the best general operating mode is for public policy-makers (with the aid of planners) to set the desired distributive pattern, but for the programs to be implemented through nonbureaucratic market or political-bargaining mechanisms.

For antipoverty programs, for example, it is possible to limit the beneficiaries of many efforts to the poor and near poor by policy fiat, but to carry out the application of the programs to the desired recipients through the use of nonbureaucratic market mechanics. One example of this can be taken from training and employment programs designed to make the poor into productive wage earners. It is possible (and is increasingly the case) for the government to designate a recipient group by low income and other characteristics and to certify specific individuals as belonging to this group, but then to turn the training itself over to the market mechanism. Government pays substantial subsidies to business for training members of the designated target groups, with the subsidies being the vehicle for inducing the market to carry out this training via the profit motive.

To the extent that the objective of the training is to decrease poverty, it would not do for the government to subsidize all training equally because the market would fail to carry out the distributive objective. Rather, the profit incentive would lead participating business firms to train those who are easiest to train because that is where the greatest profit would lie, rather than the hard-to-train poor who are the designated beneficiaries of the program's distributive objectives. But the combination of distribution designated by government and allocation left to the market seems to be a workable one. It might even be sophisticated further by providing a sliding scale of government subsidies depending on the distribution pattern desired. But the point is that distribution and efficient allocation can seldom be completely separated.

Indeed, sometimes clumsy government attempts at setting distributive patterns interfere with efficiency so badly that even the distributive benefits are largely negated. In the case of health care, for example, the major objective of the passage of the Medicare and Medicaid programs during 1964 was the distributive aim of providing more and better health care to the aged and to the poor, respectively. This was done by piling in government funds for this purpose, thus adding substantially to the total demand for medical care. Since no corresponding steps were available to increase the supply of such care in the short run, the inevitable result was that much of the government effort was dissipated in higher prices to doctors and hospitals. In the long run, this result may be ameliorated by an increase in supply of care by deliberate government efforts both to increase the number of medical personnel and to reorganize the delivery of health services, and by the long-run increase of supply ordinarily brought forth by high prices. But in the short run, the result has been pretty close to a disaster. On the other hand, some who suggest restoring allocative efficiency to the medical market do so as if allocative efficiency were the only objective; they do so essentially by attempting to restore the earlier distribution of health care in which the wealthy stood first in line and all others took what remained. Perhaps this is the only way to renew efficiency in the medical market in the short run, but if it is, it should be recognized that efficiency has been substituted for distribution as the criterion.[1]

And if considerations of allocative efficiency frequently intrude into programs intended primarily for distributional purposes, the reverse is also true. Taking defense again as a nearly pure case of a program with public objectives definable in the efficiency terms of producing the needed capability at the minimum cost (or the maximum capability for a given cost), defense also produces incomes for those who make defense goods. Changes in military programs necessarily change these incomes, and whether such distributional effects should be considered proper considerations in the making of defense policy—and the issue is debatable—realistically they are very much present. These distributional aspects affect the public decision process through political pressures and bargaining that differ from the political-distributional pressures of trade unions and Community Action programs mainly in that the defense pressures are much stronger and more effective.

Social Programs

Given all the necessary qualifications, the category of social programs in which the primary objective is redistributive but for which efficiency is also a major criterion, is a very broad one. It includes most antipoverty, manpower, education, housing, and health programs at all levels of government. For some of these programs, particularly money transfers of income to the poor, efficiency may be obtained through simplicity, as indicated below; for most, however, complexity is inherent and mechanisms must be searched out for efficient delivery.

The programs in this broad social category can be divided among three types: (1) those with complex but specific functional objectives such as training or housing; (2) those with more general objectives, such as decreasing discriminatory racial practices; and (3) those, with relatively simple and straightforward objectives, such as transfer payments.

1. For the first category, specific functional programs likely to be extremely complex in execution, the pattern of government setting the desired distribution by designating recipients

or similar means and then using some form of subsidy device to induce market forces to take the job over is a compelling one. What is done must be done carefully: for example, if the program is to be a distributive one, the distribution guidelines must be carefully set and monitored. It is too easy, for example, to point a program in the wrong direction by a false parallelism. In the case of antipoverty training programs, a parallel was drawn in 1968 between the need for human investment and the success of the investment tax credit program of 1963 in increasing the sum of capital investment in the economy. On the basis of this analogy, Senator Winston Prouty (Vermont) proposed a human investment tax credit. But the object was not parallel: it was not to increase the total investment in human capital parallel to the previous increase in total investment in physical capital; rather, it was to increase the investment in the training of specific low-income people in the population. Without such specific distributive direction, a human investment program would have failed in its purpose.

A second problem in regard to use of the market for such programs is that it should be clear that it is the market, not business expertise as such, that is the primary tool to be utilized. It is interesting to contrast two antipoverty training programs here: the Job Corps and the Job Opportunities in the Business Sector (JOBS) programs. When the Job Corps was created by the Economic Opportunity Act of 1964, a decision was made by Sargent Shriver that much of the training should be done by American industry in large centers. Throughout 1965, contracts were laboriously negotiated with such industrial giants as Litton Industries and International Telephone and Telegraph, as well as with several university consortiums. Competition did not really enter into the negotiated arrangements; what was thought to be needed was business expertise in training. And as a result of this, among other factors, the main advantage of business participation, the use of market competition to stimulate performance and to prevent complete failure by use of parallel connections, was not brought to bear. The business-run Job Corps camps were a very mixed success. None was quite so bad as a university effort at Camp Breckenridge in Kentucky; on the other hand, none was so good as a university consortium effort at Camp Gary in Texas.

In contrast to this procedure, during early 1968 the Johnson administration decided to promote large-scale business participation in training of poor adults. Rather than negotiating a few large contracts, however, the program (JOBS) was set up to provide a subsidy that, it was hoped, would induce substantial numbers of large, medium, and small businesses to participate through the market. It worked rather well, not completely up to expectations, but rather well until the 1970 recession came close to killing it for reasons having nothing to do with the effectiveness of the program. One reason it did not work better than it did was that it did not become as complete an open-market program as it might have been. The bureaucratic ethos of the Department of Labor led to the painful negotiation of each individual contract with business, and the negotiations and conditions required by the government tended to interfere with the free flow and simplicity of the market.

A well-designed tax credit program might have worked better than JOBS, simply because federal tax collectors have less of a negotiating ethos than federal contracting officers. A tax-credit system would have had its costs (the lack of negotiations would have meant that business could have gotten away with something they could not obtain under contracting), but the costs would have bought a similar and larger program. In any case, even with such drawbacks, JOBS worked better than Job Corps. The major basis of the difference was that though the JOBS program, like the Job Corps, utilized the undoubted training expertise of business, JOBS obtained its main benefit from the use of incentives in the market rather than from business expertise alone.

One improvement that might have been made in the JOBS program would have been for the government to pay for a final product—a trained and employed previously poor worker—rather than for an effort on the part of business to do the training. In normal markets, after all, those who purchase from business purchase finished products, not good tries. And there seems not too much reason why this could not be applied to such market efforts as JOBS.[2]

Indeed, the same principle might be applied to education programs. The government might (and to a limited extent is beginning to) pay firms to produce students educated according to certain standards, by whatever means. Again, if the object of such a program were compensatory education of the poor, the product to be purchased could be limited to poor students. This sort of purchase of education programs on the private market by government is an alternative, though not a mutually exclusive one, to another use of the market mechanism in the education field. The alternative would have the government provide educational grants to the families of students at the primary and secondary levels just as is done for higher education with the GI bill. These grants would then be used by the students to purchase education in any sort of institution they saw fit, subject to the same loose kind of accrediting standards applied to higher education. Grants such as this could be given out on a redistributive basis or on a uniform basis for all students. The choice between the use of the market mechanism for government purchase of educational services or for direct purchase by students should be based on the answer to the question of who can buy better education. Given the experience so far of government attempting to provide compensatory education directly to underprivileged children, there might be a presumption that the children and their families could hardly do worse by themselves.

2. The second type of broad social program has a more general objective than can be subsumed under a single functional heading such as education or manpower. Though such programs as education and manpower are parts of broad general efforts, such as those combating poverty or race discrimination, they are only partial. Such broad programs must also include less easy-to-define portions, such as community change, organization, and change in the social environment. For these fuzzier aspects of broad programs, the mechanism of economic markets does not seem appropriate; there is nothing to be bought or

sold. And indeed, even the allocation of resources among the more easily specified parts, such as education and manpower, is a distinction that would be difficult to submit to the market mechanism.

Rather, the appropriate mode here might be the political-bargaining one. To a great extent, it is both desirable and possible to carry out difficult-to-define functions and to allocate among all functions by changing the political balances that now distribute power among population groups and by allowing the political mechanism to act both on allocation and on distribution of those resources that follow on power. As has been suggested, this is the pattern that has worked so successfully in labor relations and, like use of the economic mechanism, it would seem to have a wide application. Just as it is possible in the economic case to adjust incentives to changed situations—to change the incentives for spending when a shift is needed from inflation to deflation, for example—it is possible to change balances back again or to adjust them. This was done during 1947 when the Taft-Hartley Act moved the collective bargaining balance back toward business. It was done during 1966 when the administration and Congress, feeling that the Community Action Program had moved the balance within cities too far toward the poor, restored some power to urban officialdom by passage of the Model Cities Act.

The whole question of adjustment of political balances by government action is a delicate one because it seems to imply the use of public power to affect itself and the natural tendency of power in such a situation will be to reinforce itself. This caused substantial and legitimate Congressional doubts about the use of the Community Action Program in the War on Poverty. But, in fact, government intervention to rebalance political power has been attempted in the past mainly when a clear imbalance existed, as it did in labor relations during the early 1930s and in urban affairs during the mid-1960s. And given such clear imbalances, political rebalancing has a long and substantial history in this country, beginning with the federalism of the Constitution.

3. The third category of social programs contains transfer

payments as such, particularly money payments. There is little question here of efficiency in the sense that has been discussed so far, the combining of resources to produce a result in the cheapest possible manner. But efficiency does enter in two analogous ways. First, the question of allocation among transfer payment programs, or to such programs as compared to other social programs is one to which the political-bargaining mechanism might frequently be applied. That is, if a group is intended to be the recipient of several types of programs, it would seem that this kind of decision might best be made by consultation with the group rather than by bureaucratic fiat about what allocation is right. Second, efficiency enters in the sense of efficient filling of the consumer desires of those receiving the transfers. Transfer payments are ordinarily defined to include not only money payments but also provision of various sorts of commodities and services in kind—food stamps, public housing, medicaid, and the like. If consumer sovereignty is a principle that should be applied to recipients of transfers as well as to the majority of the population, it would follow that transfers should be made in money alone and the recipient should be allowed to decide how much of this money will be spent on food, housing, medical insurance, booze, and horsebetting. Indeed, some of the suggestions above for money grants in programs such as education might be broadened even further to suggest that money that would have gone to education simply be provided in the form of transfer income, and the recipient family should be allowed to decide whether to spend that money on education or on anything else.

This last example indicates the limitations on the principle of consumer sovereignty. For many cases the social interest predominates over that of the individual's freedom to allocate his own expenditures; the social interest in transforming the children of the poor into well-educated citizens, for example, provides a reason for directing certain expenditures to education. In other cases, the importance of a certain kind of expenditure may be such that society might legitimately believe it knows better than the consumer. Substantial evidence indicates, for example, that prenatal and early childhood malnutrition have irreversible effects on the mental capabilities of victims. Society may thus legitimately demand that some portion of transfers be spent on food for mothers and children. In other cases, the market simply is not likely to work that well. Substitution of unrestricted money payments for public housing, for example, might lead in the short run mainly to a windfall for landlords, to the extent that the money was spent for housing.

In spite of these constraints, conservative (that is, nineteenth-century liberal) economists such as Milton Friedman would in fact transform virtually all government services directed to individuals into money transfer payments and allow the individuals complete freedom to spend for consumer goods, education, housing, health care (by anyone the consumer considered qualified to provide health care, without government licensing), or anything else. Most of us would not go that far, but there can be little doubt that it is easier, more efficient, and fairer to allow the recipient of transfers the right to allocate expenditures in any way he wants than it is to allocate the funds for him, unless there is an overriding reason to do so.

Consumer sovereignty as an aspect of the market mechanism thus has substantial application to the execution of transfer payments programs. Yet it would seem difficult for the market itself to distribute money transfers. It would be possible conceptually for such distribution to take place using the political-bargaining mechanism, for instance, providing Community Action or other organizations a total sum of money for distribution as they saw fit to their own constituencies. But the potential for individual and political misuse here is clearly unacceptable.

Thus, for the execution of transfer programs, governmental mechanisms as such are needed. Here, however, the problem can be simplified to the point where the governmental action necessary is virtually nondiscretionary and therefore not too subject to the faults of bureaucracy. And indeed, because it is nondiscretionary, program execution may be largely carried out by computer. In fact, in such transfer payment programs as Social Security, most of the work is computerized. Social Security is virtually nondiscretionary, and it is computerized, utilizing human beings in its execution mainly for the necessarily human function of personal contact with clients to get or disseminate information; Social Security is also perhaps the most efficient federal program in being. Certainly, it is the most successful transfer payment program.

The appeal of this sort of simplicity has been one major factor in the drive to change welfare programs from the individual-assistance, individual-distribution, individual-investigation basis on which they have been carried out since the 1930s to the impersonal basis of the so-called negative income tax as reflected in the Nixon administration's Family Assistance Program. The faults of welfare have been discussed in Chapter 3; they are in large measure consequent on the discretion of public employees following rules. The substitution of simple nondiscretionary rules for the determination of eligibility and size of payments has the potential of doing away with many of these faults. It will not necessarily come about this way; it seems entirely possible that in the zeal to give transfer payments only to those who have no other income potential, Congress will reintroduce personal investigation and discretion and, with them, most of the faults of welfare. Nonetheless, the simplicity is worth striving for.

Taxation

Moving away from social programs, the same appeal of nondiscretionary simplicity applies to the field of taxation. Taxes and transfer payments are, of course, quite similar; this similarity is the reason for the name "negative income tax" being applied to a transfer program. Indeed, in one sense, taxation can be considered a social program quite parallel to the others. The most powerful tool for achieving the desired income distribution among those above the poverty level is the income tax. This tax has the advantage of being infinitely adjustable to achieve any distribution desired. It has the market advantage of allowing the individual to decide his own allocation of the funds he has left after taxes. In this, it differs, for example, from excise taxes which distort consumer desires by raising prices for goods taxed above prices for untaxed goods.

The income tax can also have the advantages of simplicity attributed above to its negative counterpart. The potential for such simplicity exists, though, as has been seen, the federal individual income tax as applied is really two taxes: one quite simple, the other fantastically complex.

Proposals are frequently made to simplify the income tax. One such is to set a minimum income tax, allowing the taxpayer to choose whichever benefits him more, the standard complicated tax with all of its loopholes or the simple minimum which, in principle, has no loopholes. The necessity to give the taxpayer a choice between these two, however, indicates the limits of the income tax for redistributive purposes. As has been discussed, a simple loophole-free tax applying to all taxpayers would not be politically acceptable; the complexities of the tax as it is allow hidden constraints on progressivity which make the tax acceptable to politically potent upper-bracket payers.

Another tax sharing the appeal of simplicity is the general sales tax. It is easy to compute, easy to collect, and nondiscretionary. If it is really general, applying to all purchases, it also shares the appeal of nondistortion of the allocation among consumer goods. The sales tax is regressive because lower-income consumers spend more of their income on purchases and save less than people with high incomes; if food is excluded from the general sales tax, as it is in the State of California, allocative distortion is introduced, but the sales tax then picks up the added advantage of avoiding marked regressivity. Excluding food, different income groups spend roughly the same proportion of their incomes on consumer goods. In any case, the sales tax is hardly an instrument for redistribution.

The main point here, however, is not to present a general critique of the tax system but to suggest that the income tax at all levels of government, perhaps supplemented by the sales tax, is a far better instrument for revenue gathering than the property tax which is now the main support of most local governments. The property tax is bad both from the distribution and the allocative efficiency viewpoints. Because the poor spend a larger proportion of their income on housing, it is regressive. The assessment process is arbitrary and subject to all the defects of bureaucratic discretion.

Taxation is also usable and is used for a third purpose beyond revenue gathering and redistribution. It is used for applying the market mechanism to governmental regulation of private business or other individuals or groups. What is of interest here is not the extreme variety of regulation, where for legal reasons taxation is used as a means of absolute prohibition, as in the case of the gambling license tax, which, if paid by illegal gamblers, would subject them to prosecution for their illegalities. Rather, taxation is of interest as a means of setting limits on certain processes and then allocating the limited quantities by use of the market. Pollution is a case in point here. The question can be asked, "How much air and water pollution in a given area is 'tolerable'?" The answer, "None at all," is attractive but meaningless, because in a sense every human activity pollutes. What is meaningful, however, is to estimate the cost of pollution prevention at different levels and then to choose the most acceptable level of pollution and prevention costs. Given such a choice, it is then possible to allocate the tolerable pollution among polluters by use of a tax-based market mechanism. Those who value their polluting processes most highly would be willing to pay the greatest total of taxes for pollution. The producer of one good who can make his product only by causing a substantial degree of pollution and whose markets are inelastic enough that much of the cost of the tax can be passed on to his buyers will be willing to buy much more pollution than one who can change to a nonpolluting process relatively cheaply.

The same sort of principle might be applied to some other kinds of regulation. Airlines, for example, compete for routes and terminal rights, where the totals are constrained by considerations of safety and capacity. It would be possible to set these totals and to use the market by allowing lines to bid for routes and rights. This suggests one limitation on this kind of regulation by price, however. Those with the greatest ability to pay will have the greatest ability to bid. In the airlines case, distribution of income among individuals is not the issue; the big airline able to bid high may have more and poorer stockholders than the little one. But distribution of power is important, and public policy may desire to constrain the bidding process to prevent monopoly. In other similar cases, income distribution as such may be more relevant; as discussed above, some of the suggested solutions to the current crisis of medical resources go along the lines of limiting the demand for such resources to the available supply and essentially allowing bidding for this supply. But as suggested, the crisis is due to an attempt to distribute the short supply more equitably, and the proposed solution would provide efficiency at the cost of the desired distributive equity.

In addition to these cases where distribution considerations conflict with allocative ones, there are, of course, many examples of regulation in which taxes or price mechanisms simply do not apply, for example, safety regulations. Nonetheless, the principle of market allocation is so powerful in achieving efficiency that it is worth wide consideration to those fields of regulation to which it may be applicable.

Indeed, the market is so powerful a means of achieving efficiency that it would be very nice if it could be applied to the one class of government programs in which efficiency is everything and distribution has nothing to do with it. This is defense, in which the objective is still what the late Secretary of Defense Charles E. Wilson expressed as "more bang for a buck." A more sophisticated version might be "more deterrence for a dollar," but the objective of defense in achieving national military goals in the cheapest way possible is still the whole point.

Defense cannot be subject to the market mechanism because the government must have a monopoly over this variety of violent power. The same applies to some extent to local police; it still seems preferable for police services to be provided publicly rather than by vigilante organizations. In the case of police, however, both the market and distributive questions may have some relevance. The rich can and do buy their own guard services, and one might ask, "Why not encourage the policing of wealthy areas to be put on an entirely private basis?" There are some good answers to this, of course, but some moves in this direction seem inevitable and perhaps acceptable.

In any case, since the economic market mechanism does not apply to achieving efficiency in defense, nor does the idea of creating countervailing political forces, what remains is the third mode, the creative use of bureaucratic rivalry as an incentive for military men to move in desired directions. Bureaucratic rivalry aplenty, of course, exists in the military establishment, and its history provides excellent evidence that this alone does not suffice for the achievement of efficiency. The trick is to constrain such bureaucratic rivalry in two ways. (1) It is necessary to prevent oligopoly, the making of explicit or implicit deals among the services to cut up the pies of appropriations and of roles and missions. (2) The rivalry should be expressed in the right currency, the output of defense processes—military capability—rather than the inputs—soldiers and ships and airplanes.

The first needed constraint is particularly difficult to achieve; it is difficult in the military arena to prevent oligopoly by continual introduction of new bureaucratic factors. To some extent, this can be done, for example, by the building up of the Special Forces (Green Berets) during the early 1960s. In general, however, the centralized Military–Naval–Air Force Academy-based system of military oligarchy also tends to oligopoly, and the best prescription here seems to be just to keep shaking it up as much as possible, without allowing anyone to get too secure.

A degree of success in the second effort—keeping the rivalry in the right currency—was, as much as anything, the achievement of Defense Secretary McNamara and Assistant Secretaries Charles Hitch and Alain Enthoven. During 1960, the debate was still carried out in terms of "equitable distribution" of the pie among the services, a perversion of the kind of distribution discussed here. By the mid-1960s, the same discussion was carried out in terms of which services could provide the greatest capability for strategic deterrence, for delivery of tactical airpower, and so forth. It is not clear now to what extent the terminology has reverted to the earlier style, but the difference is important. If McNamara and company did make a permanent change, this was a major achievement.

While awaiting bureaucratic restructuring of the military establishment, it is prudent to assume the worst about that establishment. The lessons of Vietnam in particular indicate that solutions that may seem technically or tactically desirable will inevitably be distorted by the machinery. High-level planners must assume this distortion, rather than succumb to the temptation to choose an attractive strategy that would work really well if, just this once, it did not get twisted up. And the assumption that the seemingly attractive strategy will go sour may in turn lead to a new calculus as to participation in future Vietnam-like situations.

Federalism

Of course, general principles such as those suggested at the beginning of this chapter, must be applied in detail and with care to any specific situation or program. The argument here is that such application, involving program execution as well as idealistic concepts of what a program should look like, is the real role of the public planner. This brief survey of applications to a number of public programs is meant primarily as an illustration of a way of thinking.

But because such an illustrative procedure is necessarily selective, omitting many applications, it should be made explicit that one omission from this chapter has been deliberate, namely, the discussion of federalism, the relationships among the national government, the states, and localities. In this chapter, and indeed throughout the book, government has been treated as government, without sharp distinctions among levels. Though most of the examples here have been federal, they would seem almost as applicable to state and local governments.

The open question, however, is the possibility of utilization of state and local governments as instruments of national policy. The reason this is left open is that such an application must depend on the utilization of self-interest incentives just as in the case of economic markets, the political-bargaining mechanism, and bureaucratic competition, but we understand very little about how to even define the interests of state and local governments except in the grossest terms. What we do know is that, as in the welfare, education, and manpower cases of Chapter 3, federal-state-local systems seem to work as badly as any other highly-administered systems, and maybe worse.

So far as self-interest motivations are concerned, we know, for example, that politicians are interested in getting elected, but we do not know how this interest at the local and state levels expresses itself in governmental operations. By and large, politicians with a reputation for good government seem likely to be more electable than those without, but the question of reputation among whom, and what the ingredients of such a reputation are, are unanswered. And in a number of states, the evidence indicates that a reputation for delivering good government is irrelevant anyhow.

We also know that state and local governments are generally more responsive to special interests and to local subgroups than is the national government. Again, we do not have much idea of the operational applicability of this factor to utilization of state and local self-interest motivation to execute national policy. And again, states differ widely among themselves as to the application or meaning of this principle.

Yet a national policy executed by the states must be executed by all of them, and the differences among the states apparently mean that any program they carry out for the national government will vary so widely it would be hard to consider it a national policy at all. The belief that seems to underlie most attempts at administration of national programs through the federal system is that states and localities are by and large motivated by their view of the public interest and are more capable than the national government of applying this interest to local situations. I have no cause to challenge the depth of this public interest motivation. Indeed, this is just the point. The theme of this book has been that public interest motivations turn pernicious very easily because they lead to such a wide variety of interpretation and discretion. My contention, then, is that until we know much more about the operational implications of self-interest and public interest factors and motivations in state and local governments, we will have very little idea of how to apply national policy by utilizing the federal system. Or at least we will know one thing only, that federalism has worked badly in the past in the carrying out of national policy; there is no reason, given our current state of knowledge, to expect it to work better in the future.

It is to the quest for knowledge—the kinds of research that ought to be done to improve on the principles suggested here and create new means of effective program planning and execution—that the final chapter turns.

Notes

1. Joseph Newhouse and Vincent Taylor, in "How Should We Pay for Hospital Care?" *The Public Interest,* Spring 1971, tend, for example, to move toward efficiency at the cost of redistribution.
2. For a more detailed analysis of the JOBS program, see Robert A. Levine, *The Poor Ye Need Not Have with You: Lessons from the War on Poverty* (Cambridge: M.I.T. Press, 1970), pp. 109–116.

8

The Planner
and the Analyst

THE LAST CHAPTER treated the planner as part of the decision-making process. This direct participation is the major function for the planner in government, and without it, any kind of planning is meaningless. But the planner as decision-maker is only a partial role; the planner as policy analyst is the other major portion of the function.

Indeed, providing the linkage between decision-making and analysis is a major role of the government planner; he must inject analysis into the making of policy. Typically, in the past, this analysis has consisted mainly of laying out goals and suggesting routes to these goals. If, however, as suggested here, planning makes more sense if it is directional, laying out next steps that seem to lead to improvement, rather than ultimate-goal oriented, this changes the function of planning analysis but does not lessen its importance. It is seldom clear what next steps will lead in which direction, or whether the consequences of one alternative set of steps will be preferable to those of another. All this requires careful analysis. The planner must help with each of the three broad modes of policy execution discussed in the last chapter: use of market incentives, use of political and bargaining techniques, and encouraging bureaucratic competition. Analysis is needed to structure incentive systems so that the market mechanism will be perturbed in socially desired directions, and similar analysis is needed by the planners of political forces. Far more analysis than has been done to date on the real operating implications of bureaucratic reorganization is also required; the typical reorganization study ignores the implications of bureaucratic competition and rivalry, looking instead at organization-chart tidiness.

Within the bureaucracy, in fact, the planner should carry out a major function in promoting the constructive aspects of bureaucratic competition. For if the kind of analytical input into decision-making suggested here is to be effective, it must be carried out within the competitive processes of bureaucracy. Analysis of policy is seldom so impressively correct that it sweeps all before it; values on which plans are based differ legitimately, and so do partial assumptions. For these reasons, the best that planning can do within a bureaucracy is to raise the level of the dialogue of rivalry. As has been suggested, this, if anything, is the lasting achievement of Secretary McNamara and Assistant Secretaries Hitch and Enthoven in the Department of Defense. It may be that interservice rivalry in the future will be expressed in terms of the real demands of the defense of the United States.

All this still concerns the planner in his decision-making role. But if the planner is in some sense the bringer of rationality and analysis into the councils of government, he must also be part of another world, the analytical as well as the governmental world. And the question then is "What can analysis contribute to the process (science or art) of planning?" Yehezkel Dror has suggested the creation of a new field of policy science:

> In essence, policy-making knowledge deals with the problem of how to make policy about making policies. That is, policy-making knowledge dealing with *metapolicy*. For convenience, I will use the term *policy knowledge* to refer to both policy-issue knowledge and policy-making knowledge. *Policy* science can therefore be partly described as the discipline that searches for policy knowledge, that seeks general policy-issue knowledge and policy-making knowledge, and integrates them into a distinct study.
>
> The major problem at which policy science is directed is how to improve the design and operations of policy-making systems.[1]

Most of this book can conveniently be classed under the policy-science rubric. The remainder of this chapter briefly discusses possible future directions for the science itself in improving policy-making.

One set of questions concerns the application of policy sciences. How do the precepts suggested here, or similar precepts, apply to actual operational policy situations? Only a little study has been done in these directions. Andrew Marshall has studied bureaucratic decision-making in Soviet defense policy, concluding that the typical U.S. strategic planners' picture of the Russians as coldly rational foes has been incorrect. The Soviet defense establishment is riddled at least as much as our own by bureaucratic rivalry and received doctrine. Bringing this understanding into American defense decision-making has been the objective of the Marshall work.[2]

Another example of this kind of application of policy science is Walter Williams's study of the role of analysis and experimentation in deriving conclusions relevant to social policy-making.[3] Williams's work, like my own, is derived in large measure from experience in the analytical shop of the OEO from 1965 to 1969. Neither of the two OEO directors in this time, Sargent Shriver and Bertrand Harding, was satisfied with or even much interested in the beauty of social analysis for its own sake. Both demanded analysis that could be carried into action, and this was the beginning of thinking through the way policy recommendations could be applied, as well as what these policy recommendations should be. This was the beginning of effectiveness in planning.

Policy analysis must thus be applied to every recommendation made by the planner. Without these considerations of how the real world works, policy analysis is less than helpful. But beyond this applied analysis, far more analytical work must be done on the basic rules of planning, decision-making, and implementation. To make one obvious point, the principles suggested here are undoubtedly oversimplified and by no means sacrosanct. Much more work along these lines is needed; what policy systems are really likely to be effective in what ways?

In addition, much more generalization is needed about the application of these principles or others like them. Some of the questions needing investigation border on the ethics of the planning role. For example, what part of what decision-making apparatus should the planner or analyst try to affect directly by the beauty of his argument? What decision-makers should he assume are outside the net of his logic, part of the problem to be affected manipulatively rather than part of the solution? The part-of-the-problem group would include those decision-makers who are impervious to or unreachable by the rationality of the planner's arguments or those who simply hold values different from those underlying the planning recommendations.

On the one hand, every decision-maker (or at least every decision-maker within American government structures) might be treated in planning analysis as a rational, reachable individual, with all proceeding from the same set of values, so that the planner is best advised to lay out his recommendations for the national good and to count on their rationality to convince all the necessary actors. The PPB system came close to this, assuming a community of interest not only among federal operating agencies, the Budget Bureau, and the administration, but also of the states, localities, and quasi-public instrumentalities. In doing this, it denied for practical purposes the validity of the kind of competitive process that, it has been suggested, really pervades the bureaucracy. This was a major limitation of program budgeting as it was operated.

But if complete rationality and community of interest is one polar assumption, and a questionable one, it becomes difficult to decide how far from this pole we should move. It is too easy to reach the other extreme, where the planner considers every decision-maker an object of manipulation to be approached more through his subconscious than through conscious rationality. This is what Kathleen Archibald terms "the clinical approach," utilized, for example, by psychologists trying to affect foreign policy by manipulating the underlying motivations of the executors of this policy.[4] At best, this tends to be arrogant and undemocratic; at worst, it can also be ineffective because policy-makers operate much more at the rational level than these behavioral scientists sometimes give them credit for.

Between these two extremes of manipulation and assumed complete rationality lie a variety of cases. It would seem reasonable in advising makers of American foreign policy, for example, to take foreign decision-makers, even allies, as best approachable through such techniques as honest bargaining, rather than assuming a broad community of interest in which all that needs to be done is devise the most rational analytical approach to common goals. In the Chapter 4 discussion of NATO planning during the early and mid-1960s, for instance, it was suggested that a major American error was to assume an overriding common interest of NATO members in defense against a massive Soviet attack, that American NATO planning would have worked much better had we assumed a variety of individual national interests among which such defense was only one (and a minor one at that, considering the improbability of massive attack). Then we could have devised bargains among allies that might have worked much better than did the long debates on the military aspects of such concepts as the Multilateral Nuclear Force, and the "trip-wire." Few people really believed that the "optimal" solutions derived from these debates would really change policy. They were debates over the wrong questions. It would have made far more sense to treat the British, French, and Germans as bargaining partners with many common interests and some opposing ones.

In matters contained within American governmental structures, the position of the planner must determine to a great extent the style of his advice. As an intimate within-government adviser, the planner must consider the particular decision-maker being advised as depending mainly on planning rationality; to do otherwise would be to abdicate the planner's role of injecting rational analysis. But other decision-makers in other departments may legitimately be considered data: "If we present this recommendation, Secretary X's reaction is likely to be as follows." As the adviser becomes less intimately associated with any decision-maker (in the outer rings of university and other extragovernmental analysts), however, the governmental structure can increasingly be treated as being made up of rational people not to be manipulated. And so forth; the point here is not to create a complete set of ethics but to suggest that such ethical considerations as these deserve serious explicit consideration in any analysis of the role of public planning.

One more related ethical consideration that should be mentioned briefly is that of the "social myth." In many such cases as the ones discussed here, if the alternatives are publicly discussed in the relatively cold-blooded terms used here, the possibility of accomplishing anything will be largely dissipated. Using the NATO case again, were we to try to devise a plan based on British, French, German, and so forth motives, and were it indicated that these motives had little to do with the explicit defense-against-the-Soviets rationale for NATO, the whole thing might collapse rather quickly. On the record, the United States keeps some hundreds of thousands of troops in Europe to defend against Soviet attack; off the record, at least during the early 1960s, the main reason for American forces in Europe was to keep Western Europe stable by satisfying West German security feelings. Yet, were the latter to be admitted, it would become impossible to keep the troops there; defense against the Soviets was what made policy politically viable. A "social myth" need not be completely or even mostly mythical. It may have a high truth content; nonetheless, it is defined as an organizing principle for gaining support, and neither high nor low truth content is a necessary part of that definition. Soviet attack was at one time a very real fear; certainly the fear is not nonexistent now. But the point is that it is a viable social myth so long as it is believed enough to create the kind of support necessary for the policy.

A similar example can be taken from the Community Action programs discussed here. It has been suggested that the real function of Community Action has been to rebalance political bargaining power in favor of the poor. But this is not really an acceptable principle to many people, including many Congressmen, and for this reason, it is seldom talked about officially. What has been talked about in the past has been community planning because planning of this type has been politically acceptable. But such planning has not worked well, if at all, and the use of this particular social myth may thus be outliving its major function. Given that such rebalancing of political forces continues to be a necessity, some new myth may be needed: community economic development may be the coming one.

Again, the ethics of the above cases need careful study. The use of social myths is a manipulative technique and not a terribly tasteful one. I was reminded of this early in the current study when I was discussing it with a group of students who were shocked by the manipulative and elitist implications of utilizing social myths. They may well have been right, yet such techniques are used all the time. More analysis is needed of the ethics involved; perhaps we need a social myth about the use of social myths.

All this, however, is somewhat premature, because we do not really know enough yet to be dangerous manipulators. We know a good deal about the market system as it operates; economics is by far the most advanced of the behavioral sciences in its relation to policy. We probably know enough about the market system to be able to manipulate incentives for the social purposes we desire. To some extent, we know about politics and about intergroup bargaining. The literature of politics is a rich one, and bases for understanding bargaining have been laid down by Schelling and others. Here, too, we probably know enough to manipulate forces and incentives in desirable directions.

But much (probably most) public policy will continue to be carried out by public bureaucracies, and the manipulation of such bureaucracies is a vast unexplored area, resembling the continent of Africa during mid-nineteenth century. As has been discussed, good descriptive works exist, but to the extent that they become prescriptive, the prescriptions are usable only at a much lower level of aggregation and of policy-making than that which is the target here. Nor does any coherent generalizable theory of bureaucracy exist, from which normative prescriptions can be deduced. This study has largely dodged the issues of bureaucracy, saying merely that bureaucracy and planning have not worked and suggesting several ways around bureaucracy. There have been some mild suggestions, based on inductive reasoning, that perhaps a greater degree of competition within the bureaucracy would help reach public objectives more effectively. But how to motivate bureaucracies has been ignored, other than the suggestion for further competition.

What is needed now is detailed inductive and deductive study of bureaucracies of various sorts. Studies should investigate the motivations of both individual bureaucrats and bureaucratic organizations at a level of detail and precision sufficient to estimate how changing incentives will lead through motivations to predictable changes of behavior. In other words, what is needed is a theory that can be applied to actual cases. We need a general theory and we need specific subtheories for federal civil and military bureaucracies. Until those who draw policy recommendations understand well enough how these recommendations will go through the machine and what will come out, the danger of more Vietnams will be high. Until similar understanding is gained for the civil bureaucracy, ineffective policy execution will remain routine and extrabureaucratic devices will have to be pressed to or beyond their natural limits.

Even less known, and perhaps even more important to be known, are the individual and group motivations that affect the multitude of organizations and subgroups ordinarily lumped together as state and local government. We have little operational knowledge of the motivations and incentives of state politicians at the many levels at which they operate. We have even less knowledge of what moves or can move appointed civil service bureaucrats at all these various levels. All we really know inductively is Murphy's Law, that anything that can go wrong will. And this helps very little. Until we have much more knowledge and applicable theory, enough to predict consequences of policies impinging on states and localities, much of the talk of creative federalism will be specious. It will remain what for the most part it is now, either a dodge of responsibility on the part of the federal government or an effort to put things at a level where it is known that special interests have more power (for one thing that is known is that these interests currently do have far more power at local levels than nationally). In any case, the national policy system is incomplete because of the lack of effective bringing in of states and localities; it will remain incomplete until we have the knowledge to bring them in effectively.

I conclude on one final point. Looked at coldly and objectively, policy is almost always very very ineffective. Lindblom's basic message is that very little can be done anyhow, so we might as well sit back and enjoy the system. In order to believe otherwise, we must to some extent suspend one disbelief or another. The norm for policy planners is to suspend what should be the prudent disbelief that a plan can go through the system with its implementation coming out anywhere near the reasonable expectations of the planner.

The purpose of this book, however, might be termed an attempt to suspend another sort of disbelief. My own disbelief that the distortions of the bureaucratic machine will not change everything around is too strong to be suspended; therefore, I contend that we must both get around the machine and learn how to change it. But, as has been pointed out to me, this in turn requires the suspension of the disbelief that any schemes such as the ones suggested here can be put through our creaky political machinery: the executive and legislative machinery of the federal government, the similar machinery of states and localities, and the largely hidden machinery of private special interests that benefit from the failure to reach socially agreed-on objectives.

Given this degree of pessimism, why this book at all? For two reasons. First, it is not literally true that no planned policy prescription ever works. Statistically, some do. Since we never know in advance which plans will be the successes, this fact alone gives little operational support for any system of planning. But if, through suggestions of the nature set forth here, the number can be changed—from 5 percent to 10 percent or from 20 percent to 30 percent, depending on one's assumption about the current baseline—this would be a major achievement. And it might not take too much suspension of belief to think that this could be possible. Second, the one point at which we must suspend disbelief, if we are to continue with our present form of government, is in the ability of the political system to make changes. If the political system cannot be induced to make changes of the sort suggested here (not necessarily these changes, perhaps entirely different ones stemming from parallel but better analysis), there is no hope left at all. And this is a point I have not yet reached. This disbelief, I still suspend.

Notes

1. Yehezkel Dror, *Public Policymaking Reexamined* (San Francisco: Chandler Publishers, 1968), p. 8.
2. Andrew Marshall, unpublished memoranda.
3. Walter Williams, *Social Policy Research and Analysis: The Experience in the Federal Agencies* (New York: American Elsevier, 1971).
4. Kathleen Archibald, "Three Views of the Expert's Role in Policymaking: Systems Analysis, Incrementalism, and the Clinical Approach," *Policy Sciences* (1970), 1:1.

Index

Aid to Families with Dependent Children (AFDC), 62, 63, 66
Alinsky, Saul, 96
Allison, Graham, 138–139
allocation, resource, 175; distribution compared to, 167–168, 170–171; and NRA, 76; and pollution, 180; and taxation, 43–44, 178–180; and transfer payments, 176–177; and wartime price controls, 77–80
Anderson, Martin, 85; quoted, 83–84
Anshen, Melvin: quoted, 80–81
Archibald, Kathleen, 189
Argyris, Christopher, 150
Armed Services Committee, House of Representatives Special Subcommittee: quoted, 117–118

bargaining: collective, 23, 72–74, 86–95, 101–102; political, 23, 101–102, 136, 166, 168, 169, 171, 175–177, 191, 192
Bennis, Warren: quoted, 150–151
bombing, strategic, 109, 128–129
Budget, Bureau of the, 5, 96, 98
bureaucracy, 10–15, 24, 133–141, 192–194; defined, 11–12; military, 120, 127, 143–145; monopoly in, 142–143, 168, 181; and program budgeting, 143–150, 152–153. *See also* competition: bureaucratic; Organization Development
business cycle, 20, 31–41, 71–72